THE LIFE OF FAITH

THE LIFE OF FAITH

WILLIAM ROMAINE

BAKER BOOK HOUSE
Grand Rapids, Michigan

Reprinted 1981 by
Baker Book House Company
from the edition published by
George Routledge and Sons

ISBN: 0-8010-7704-4

PHOTOLITHOPRINTED BY CUSHING - MALLOY, INC.
ANN ARBOR, MICHIGAN, UNITED STATES OF AMERICA

THE LIFE

OF THE

REV. WILLIAM ROMAINE

THE excellent author of the following sheets was born at Hartlepool, in the county of Durham, September 25, 1714. It appears from the most authentic account of him published, that his father was one of the unfortunate emigrants, who issued from a colony in France, during the distracted reign of Louis XIV. upon the revocation of the edict of Nantes. In this town he became a member of the corporation, which is a very ancient one. Here he settled, and for his means of subsistence became a corn-dealer; and as he was a man fearing God and hating covetousness, that canker of the human mind, he gave a remarkable proof of his benevolent disposition in the year 1741.

England was then at war with Spain; and, as wartime usually occasions an advance in the price of most necessaries, wheat was then advanced from six to fifteen shillings per bol, the bushel of that place, containing about two of the common measures of Winchester. This occasioned the people to be much displeased, and they soon rose in a very tumultuous manner in great numbers, and became very troublesome at Hartlepool. Mr. Romaine now became a mediator; and to put an effectual stop to their complaints, actually sold all the corn he was possessed of at five shillings a bushel, while the other corn-merchants of the place refused to part with a sack upon such moderate terms.

In this manner, with the blessings of the poor, and without reproach from any, he brought up a family of two sons and three daughters, whom he lived to see comfortably and respectably, settled in the world. He lived to the age of eighty-five, and was "gathered to the Lord" in the year 1757.

Our author was the second son, and his promising disposition inclined his parents to send him very early to the Grammar School at Houghton le Spring, in the county of Durham, founded by the celebrated rector of that parish, Barnard Gilpin; here he remained seven years, whence he removed to Oxford about 1731. He was first at Hertford College, but afterward removed to Christ Church; there the Rev. Mr. Fifield Allen was his tutor, who was afterward chaplain to Bishop Gibson, of the see of London, archdeacon of Middlesex, sub-dean of the Royal Chapel, a prebendary of St. Paul, and well known to most classical scholars as being the editor of the three "Electras" used in the school of Westminster. His residence was principally at Oxford, till he took up his degree of Master of Arts, which commenced on the 15th of October, 1737, having been previously ordained a deacon at Hertford the year before by the then bishop of that see, Dr. H. Egerton. After he had obtained orders, he was appointed to the curacy of Loe Trenchard, near Lidford, in Devonshire, which he filled but a few months, for on the 15th day of December in the same year, he was ordained a priest by the then bishop of Winchester, Dr. Benjamin Hoadley, who obtained for him a nomination to the church of Banstead, which he served for some years, together with that of Horton, in Middlesex, officiating as curate to Mr. Edwards, who had both those livings.

It was at this place he had the happiness to become acquainted with Sir Daniel Lambert, who had a country-house there, an alderman of London, and who, serving the mayoralty in 1741, appointed Mr. Romaine his chaplain, which opened him the way into the cathedral of St. Paul, where he preached the second sermon that he printed, on the 14th and 15th verses of Rom. chap. ii., in which may be discovered the sound classical divine, with the religion of a believing heart.

The first sermon which he printed was preached before the University of Oxford, March 4, 1739; and the third upon the same subject, and at the same place, St. Mary's, in Oxford, was printed the beginning of 1742; they are upon the subjects of Future Rewards and Punishments, proved to be the sanctions of the Mosaic dispensation, in answer to "Warburton's Divine Legation of Moses," two volumes of which had then made their appearance. Those who wish to learn more of this controversy, are referred, for information, to the second volume of the "Works of the Learned," for 1739, where are to be found Mr. Romaine's original correspondence with Dr. Warburton, and the whole of that dispute, arranged by Dr. Birch, the editor, afterward librarian to the British Museum.

He had now engaged in the arduous undertaking of preparing for the press a new edition of "Calasio's Concordance;" a work which employed him seven years, and he published the first volume in 1747.

This is a work highly celebrated abroad, and how far he may be justified or censured for having omitted his author's account of the word Elohim, which is usually rendered GOD, and having substituted his own in the stead, is left to the learned to decide; certain it is, that with the credit of restoring to light one of the most useful works that ever was published, he has ventured a criticism which his warmest advocates can but reluctantly defend. But he has excused himself, by imputing himself criminal, if he had acted otherwise. His alteration is marked by inverted commas; and by this apology he must stand or fall in the public opinion. He is now supposed to have meant to return home; but on accidentally meeting with a gentleman, a total stranger to him, just as he was going to embark for his passage, on a visit to his own country, he procured him a very beneficial, and at the same time unlooked-for, establishment in the church, for we often find, that while "man proposes, God disposes."

This was a friend, who, though unknown to him, from his knowledge of his father resolved upon serving him in some essential way, and having much interest, offered him the lectureship of the united parishes of St. George's, Botolph-lane, and St. Botolph, Billingsgate. To this proposal he consented, and postponed his intended voyage; but he made his conditions, that he should not be obliged to canvass in person, according to the vulgar method, which from principle he always declined, as he thought it most unworthy of the Christian character.

This happened in 1748, when he was chosen in the lectureship of the above-mentioned places; and he is recorded among the promotions in the "Gentleman's Magazine" for November, of that year, as the editor of "Calasio's Dictionary."

From the contents of some of his private letters about this time, he seems to own that he was much infected with worldly pride, and with the sufficiency of his own merits; but he soon took Timothy's advice, and became more sober-minded, reflecting that the enticing things of this world are but the outward man, while the excellency of a gracious spirit exceedeth all things.

In 1749, he was chosen lecturer of St. Dustan-in-the-West, to which was united another, endowed by Dr. White, for the Benchers of the Temple; but the first was a common parish lecture, supported by voluntary subscriptions. Our author was appointed to both, and continued a long while in the quiet exercise of both, till his faithful discharge of them raised him some enemies, whose violent clamour and opposition ended in the most shameful abuse and personal affronts. The rector, who had a long while viewed Mr. Romaine with a very jealous eye, for the large congregations which usually attended him, thought fit at last to dispute with him the right of the pulpit, and assumed the right of filling it during the time of prayers, in order to exclude him from it.

This affair became, at last, so serious, that it was carried into the Court of the King's Bench, in 1762, where Lord Mansfield's decision was, that Mr. Romaine should retain Dr. White's lectureship, with the old salary of 18*l.* a year, to be exercised at seven in the evening; the churchwardens then refused to let the church be opened till that hour, and to light it when there was occasion; so that our divine frequently read prayers and preached by the light of a single candle, which he held in his own hand, the church-doors remaining shut until the precise time fixed by the law for delivering the lecture, the congregation all the while waiting in the street.

It was in this situation of things one evening that Dr. Terrick, the then bishop of London, who had been Mr. Romaine's predecessor in the lectureship, happening to pass by, inquired among the crowd the cause of the meeting; and being informed it was the audience of Dr. White's lecture delivered by Mr. Romaine, who were in this predicament, he considered the circumstance, and immediately undertook to interfere with the rector and the parish, and obtained for him and his hearers the use of the church, for prayers to begin at six o'clock, and proper lights to be provided for the winter season. These measures settled the dispute, and he remained quietly in the exercise of his ministry there until his latter end.

Mr. Romaine was appointed assistant morning preacher in 1750, to the parish of St. George, Hanover Square. This office is not a settlement, but only optional and dependent on the opinion of the rector, who called him to the office and also removed him from it. This was Dr. A. Trebeck; the first act was the result of friendship, and the latter of displeasure at his popularity and plainness of preaching, for all his discourses were of Christ alone, and Christ crucified. He retired from this office in 1755; during his exercise in which he had occasionally preached at Bow Church, in the room of Dr. Newton, afterward bishop of Bristol, but then rector of that parish, and lecturer of St. George's, Hanover Square, and also at Curzon Chapel, then known by the name of St. George's Chapel, May Fair, in exchange with Dr. Trebeck himself, who was the morning preacher of the chapel.

Some time about this period he was called to the professorship of astronomy in Gresham College; but he was more a divine than a philosopher, and having but an indifferent opinion of the Newtonian philosophy, he opposed it with firmness, and observing in the calculations of the day a difference of 121,000,000 of miles, so he compared the modern divinity as bringing up souls as many miles short of heaven. The only remains that can be met with of his conduct in his professorship, I believe are to be read in the March number of the "Gentleman's Magazine" for 1752.

While his mind was thus busied with the philosophy of the world, his heart was still occupied with the promises of God; and what he lost with man, he obtained tenfold with his Maker.

The famous Jew Naturalization Bill was now the subject of public consideration; and those who opposed it were highly gratified by the part he took in that perilous business, and on which occasion he published a pamphlet, which was afterwards reprinted in 1753. In 1755 our author changed his condition by marrying Miss Price, whom he left an affectionate widow. Soon after his leaving his situation at St. George's, Hanover Square, he became curate and morning preacher at St. Olave's, Southwark; this was the beginning of 1756, and here he continued to 1759; and to this congregation he dedicated his sermon upon Ezekiel's dry bones, preached in their church, and published at their desire. He did not reside long in the rectory-house before he removed to a pleasant situation in Walnut-tree Walk, Lambeth.

He used in the early part of his life to be very severe with the luxurious manner of living of the modern dignitaries of the church, and which gave great offence, but he left this off by degrees; as did also, at the same time, the Rev. George Whitfield, who, particularly in the latter part of his life, began to grow very corpulent.

After he had relinquished the cure of St. Olave's, he was for near two years morning preacher at St. Bartholomew's the Great, near West Smithfield; and from thence went to Westminster Chapel, where he held the same office for six months, till the dean and chapter thought proper, upon his great popularity, to withdraw their patronage and protection from him, and refused him their nomination for a licence to preach there. He had now no other establishment in the church, excepting the lectureship of St. Dunstan-in-the-West, till he was chosen to the rectory of Blackfriars, in 1764; and then, owing to a dispute relating to his advancement, that was afterwards settled in the Court of Chancery, he was not fixed in it before the year 1766.

During this interval he was not idle; he preached many charity sermons in several churches in and about London; and with truth it may be asserted that he brought better collections than his contemporaries by their mere essays upon charity.

He was also during this interval strongly solicited to fill the pulpit of St. Paul's Church, in Philadelphia, to which was appended a salary of 600*l*. a year; and these offers were seconded by the most urgent and repeated entreaties of Mr. Whitfield, his friend, who considered him as persecuted in one city, which plainly directed him to go to another; but he was a thorough churchman, and for particular reasons, which he never imparted, he declined all thoughts of going there, although he considered many who had retired to that part of the world as rightly disposed as himself in keeping in England.

His attention at this time was particularly taken up with his favourite publication, "The Life of Faith," the first edition of which came out about this time.

We now enter upon the detail of a few circumstances relating to his transactions in his memorable appointment to his last settlement as to this world, in the rectory of St. Andrew-by-the-Wardrobe, and St. Ann's, Blackfriars. Nor were the ways of Providence less wonderful in this part of his life than they had been before. It appears that the right of presentation to this living is alternately by the crown and the parishioners. The late incumbent was a Mr. Henley, a nephew of the then Lord Chancellor Henley. He died while a young man, of a putrid fever, which he caught of one of his parishioners at a visit, after holding the place only about six years and a half. It was now the turn of the parish to nominate, and Mr. Romaine was spoken of as a fit person to fill such an important station, and he was accordingly proposed, without his knowledge or consent; for the first intimation he received of it was from a newspaper, which he happened to read by accident while on a journey. Some persons, who did not wish him so well, spread a rumour that he would be above soliciting their votes and interest. But upon the day appointed for the candidates to preach their probationary sermon, Mr. Romaine made his appearance among them; this was the 30th of September, 1764. Upon this occasion many of his friends absented themselves, who had always been in the habit of hearing him, lest they should crowd the church, and occupy the seats of the inhabitants; and by giving them offence, throw obstacles in the way of his election.

In his sermon he made a handsome apology for not canvassing in person, and this operated greatly in his favour; it was well received by the parishioners, and published at their request.

Yet he had some opposition to withstand, for there were two other candidates for the living besides himself, one named Warner, and the other Smith, and a scrutiny was demanded. However, this scrutiny did not produce any decision. The parish were divided about what should constitute the proper qualification of an elector; and a second election was agreed upon by the friends of both, which ended in favour of our divine, who had a great majority of votes, and was declared duly elected. But the other side still remained dissatisfied, and put in another claim, which occasioned the matter to be transferred into the Court of Chancery, where it continued for more than a year, and about the beginning of 1766 a decree was granted by Lord Chancellor Henley in favour of Mr. Romaine. He was accordingly inducted into the office, but was observed to tremble much during the ceremony. He was conscious, undoubtedly, of the heavy weight of his office, but it was his Master's will, he observed to one of his friends who wrote to him upon the occasion; and he entered upon his living not only in the faith and patience of Christ, but also with a considerate and decided preference to the Church of England, in which he determined to preach His name and wonderful salvation.

It was about this time he published his "Walk of Faith," in two volumes, 12mo. He was not careless of his temporal affairs, although the spiritual took up most of his attention. The parsonage-house being unfit to live in, having occasionally been converted into warehouses, he prevailed upon the inhabitants to cause it to be taken down, and he built a handsome rectory-house close to the church for himself and his posterity. He also prevailed upon the inhabitants to repair the church, and to erect a gallery at the west end of it, for the convenience of his increasing congregation, and to demolish the high wall that surrounded it, by which means it became one of the best places of public worship in London. After these necessary alterations were made, he prevailed upon his congregation to make a subscription toward defraying the expenses, that the parishioners might not have to complain that his accommodation brought expenses upon them. In this he was successful: £500 were raised by voluntary gifts; and this instance of his generosity to the parish is recorded by the following inscription over the west door:—

This Church was Repaired and Beautified,

A.D. MDCCLXXIV.,

At the expense of the United Parishes, and the generous Contribution of the Congregation.

The Rev. WILLIAM ROMAINE, M.A.,

Rector of St. Andrew by the Wardrobe, and of St. Ann's, Blackfriars.

| CHARLES GRIFFITHS, | JOHN HOLTON, |
| THOMAS COOK, | JOHN DAVIS. |

CHURCHWARDENS.

Love as Brethren.

Mr. Romaine was a great benefactor to his parishes, as a promoter of charity. Every call of distress, both public and private, urged his warmest exhortations, and the sums raised were generally proportionate to the motives urged. The yearly collections for the poor of the parish and the schools in the ward, with the money collected in the church at the weekly sacraments, which he was the first to promote, and with the charity sermons which he preached, amounted one year with another to 300*l.* a year. Even the pew-openers, who were but two at first, when he died were increased to eight, each getting a comfortable livelihood from the congregation, without any assistance from the parish.

When the great fire happened in Blackfriars, in 1793, which consumed many of the houses, containing a number of poor families upon every floor, he was the first to alleviate their distress on this occasion. He caused one of the inhabitants to relieve the sufferers with two guineas each, to the amount of more than ninety guineas, for which sum he made himself debtor to that gentleman.

His zeal upon this public calamity was long remembered. On the mornings of the Sunday and Tuesday following, he pleaded from the pulpit for the poor sufferers, who had been entirely ruined by this shocking disaster. The sum he raised, inclusive of a donation of 50*l.* from the Duke of York, amounted to upwards of 300*l.* He, besides this, prevailed upon the inhabitants of Ludgate to lend their assistance upon this occasion, which, together with the former collection, enabled him to give from 10*l.* to 18*l.* each to the sufferers.

When the calamities of the poor French emigrants called upon the national generosity and public spirit, he was no less zealous in their behalf; on which account some evil-minded persons, mistaking the motive, in an anonymous pamphlet charged him with favouring the Roman Catholic religion, as if relieving the distresses of a papist, whom compulsive necessities had forced upon us for charity, was encouraging the errors of popery.

Many public charities lost a good and firm benefactor in Mr. Romaine: but in a more especial degree the Royal Humane Society. Convinced of the utility of this institution, he delivered a voluntary sermon for their relief, at Blackfriars, in the year 1777; observing, that, by those means, the soul might have the benefit as well as the body; for, he observed, their miraculous recovery made them serious, and their thoughtfulness brought them to inquire how it might have been with them, had they then been precipitated into eternity. Mr. Romaine preached annually for this Society for seventeen years, and his sermons brought in generally about thirty pounds, besides some new subscribers.

The Bible Society also experienced the benefit of his pious exertions. He observed, much good was done by it, both by sea and land.

The life of Mr. Romaine had very little to do with the men of the present evil generation, or, as they are called, the men of the world. He lived regularly useful in his vocation. He usually resided in London, or near it, from the commencement of November term, until the long vacation after Trinity term, when he generally took a little excursion into the country, which was always northward while his mother lived, and afterward, chiefly into the west, where he had many friends. He seldom suffered himself to remain silent on the Lord's-day, and his Bible was his companion regularly every day, which he constantly read through once a year.

He was not without misfortunes in his family. He suffered the severe mortification of losing his second son, who was a captain in the military service of the East-India Company. This event happened at Trincomalee, in June, 1782. And what is remarkable, he preached, notwithstanding, the same evening he received the account of his son's death, contrary to his wife's advice; but he replied, that he durst not leave his Master's concerns unattended to on that account.

He was most admirable in the management of his time. He constantly breakfasted at six in the morning, dinner was always ready for him at half-past one, and he supped at seven in the evening. He assembled his family to prayers at nine in the morning, and at the same hour at night, and occasionally his friends were admitted to these private devotions. His Hebrew Psalter was his constant breakfast companion. From ten to one he was employed in visiting the sick, and his friends. His studies occupied the most part of the afternoon, and he sometimes resumed the exercise of walking after supper, in the height of summer, and retired to rest always at ten. From this mode of life he never deviated, but when at a friend's house.

He had long been in the constant habit of friendship with the poor, unfortunate Dr. Dodd; but that gentleman having once expressed some dislike at Mr. Romaine's conduct and strictness, a coolness ensued; but when that unhappy man was in Newgate, for the crime for which he suffered, Mr. Romaine visited him there; their conversation there, as a friend has communicated it, equally evinced Mr. Romaine's abhorrence of sin and pity for sinners.

It is lamented by many good Christians, that for the sake of posterity, he did not keep a diary, or commit more of his thoughts, and the occurrences of his life, to writing. But among all his papers, only one of this sort was found, entitled, "An Old Man," and written on the day he accomplished the age of seventy years. The last years of his life seem to have taken their turn from this day; and he has very aptly drawn his own character, when describing the triumph of faith over the infirmities of age. "He walked in the steps of the faith of Abraham, and brought forth more fruit in his age, till he died an old man, and full of days, satisfied with all that was past, all that was present, and all that was before him."

To the fatal time, which put a period to his mortal career, he constantly pursued his ministerial labours, which, with his summer excursions, he used merrily to call his summer and winter campaigns; thus he kept the field like a good soldier to the last. His last illness commenced on the 6th of June, which put an end to his life and labours on the 26th of July. He was very sensible it was his last illness, and he considered it so from the moment he was taken; and though at intervals he had faint symptoms of a probable recovery, yet he never more attempted to resume his ministerial functions.

He expressed a deal of anxiety, affection, and kindness

for his partner, Mrs. Romaine; and after thanking her for all her care, he would bless her, and make frequent mention of her in his prayers.

His illness continued to bring him lower and lower, until Sunday, July, 26, 1795, when he expired, uttering some precious words of the gospel. Thus lived, and thus piously resigned his breath, the Rev. William Romaine. It was not the design of his friends and surviving relations to make any show of his funeral; but all their efforts for privacy were vain; he was too much in the mind of the people, for such an intention to take place.

On Monday, the 3rd of August, 1795, the corpse was removed from Mr. Whiteridge's house, where he died, to be interred in the rectory-vault, in Blackfriars-church. The funeral procession began to move about eleven o'clock in the forenoon, and was joined by fifty coaches on Clapham-common; the numbers on foot, who surrounded and followed, were incredible. At Blackfriars-bridge, the children of the charity-school, with the beadle, waited to join the procession. The city marshals and their men met it also, by order of the lord mayor, as a token of respect to his memory.

The church, which was previously hung in black, was filled with people, many of whom were dressed in black. The funeral service was performed by the Rev. Mr. Goode, to a very numerous and affected audience. Three funeral sermons were preached on the Lord's-day following, and a monument has been erected to his memory in his own church.

His character has suffered something from the imputation of asperity; but those who judged of him hastily did not know him. He is said to have abruptly answered to the inquiries of his friends in the street; as once, when Dr. G. and Mr. J. met him in Cheapside, the latter asked our divine, "if he had forgotten him," to which Mr. Romaine made reply, "that he had not, nor his Master neither." This, if properly understood, carries no cynical air with it, as has been misrepresented in print, by altering the mode of the inquiry, thus, "Mr.

Romaine, do you know me?" in which case, the same answer had a direct opposite sense, viz. that he did not, nor his master neither.

It has been observed of him, that he was an example to believers, in holiness of life, in universal benevolence, in faith, and in every good work.

Thus that much-honoured servant of Christ, William Romaine, lived, and thus he died, leaving us an example to follow his steps.

THE
LIFE OF FAITH

THE
LIFE OF FAITH

The persons for whose use this little tract is drawn up, are supposed to be practically acquainted with these following truths: they have been convinced of sin, and convinced of righteousness. The word of God has been made effectual by the application of the Holy Spirit to teach them the nature of the divine law; and upon comparing their hearts and their lives with it, they have been brought in guilty. They found themselves fallen creatures, and they felt the sad consequences of the fall, namely, total ignorance in the understanding of God and his ways, an open rebellion against Him in the will, and an entire enmity in the heart, a life spent in the service of the world, the flesh, and the devil; and on all these accounts guilty before God, and by nature children of wrath. When they were convinced of those truths in their judgments, and the awakened conscience sought for ease and deliverance, then they found they were helpless and without strength. They could take no step, nor do anything, which could in the least save them from their sins. Whatever method they thought of, it failed them upon trial, and left conscience more uneasy than before. Did they purpose to repent? They found such a repentance as God would be pleased with, was the gift of Christ. He was exalted to be a Prince and a Saviour to give repentance. Suppose they thought of reforming their lives, yet what is to become of their old sins? Will present obedience, if it could be perfectly paid, make any atonement for past disobedience? Will the broken law take part of our duty for the whole? No. It has determined, that whosoever shall keep the whole law, and yet offend in one point, he is guilty of all. And let him be ever so careful in doing what the law requires, or in avoiding what the law forbids, let him fast and pray and give alms, hear and read the word, be early and late at ordinances, yet the enlightened conscience cannot be herewith satisfied; because by these duties he cannot undo the sin committed, and because he will find so many failings in them, that they will be still adding to his guilt and increasing his misery.

What method then shall he take? The more he strives to make himself better, the worse he finds himself. He sees the pollution of sin greater. He discovers more of its guilt. He finds in himself a want of all good, and an inclination to all evil. He is now convinced, that the law is holy, just, and good; but when he would keep it, evil is present with him. This makes him deeply sensible of his guilty, helpless state, and shows him that by the works of the law he cannot be saved. His heart, like a fountain, is continually sending forth evil thoughts, yea, the very imaginations of it are only and altogether evil, and words and works partake of the nature of that evil fountain from whence they flow; so that, after all his efforts, he cannot quiet his conscience nor attain peace with God.

The law having done its office, as a schoolmaster, by convincing him of these truths, stops his mouth, that he has not a word to say, why sentence should not be passed upon him. And there it leaves him, guilty and helpless. It can do nothing more for him, than show him that he is a child of wrath, and that he deserves to have the wrath of God abiding upon him for ever: for by the law is the knowledge of sin.

The gospel finds him in this condition, as the good Samaritan did the wounded traveller, and brings him good news. It discovers to him the way of salvation contrived in the covenant of grace, and manifests to him what the ever blessed Trinity had therein purposed, and what in the fulness of time was accomplished. That all the perfections of the Godhead might be infinitely and everlastingly glorified, the Father covenanted to gain honour and dignity to his law and justice, to his faithfulness and holiness, by insisting upon man's appearing at his bar in the perfect righteousness of the law. But man having no such righteousness of his own, all having sinned, and there being none righteous, no not one; how can he be saved? The Lord Christ, a person in the Godhead co-equal and co-eternal with the Father, undertook to be his Saviour. He covenanted to stand up as the head and surety of his people, in their nature and in their stead, to obey for them, that by his infinitely precious obedience many might be made righteous, and to suffer for them, that by his everlasting meritorious stripes they might be healed. Accordingly, in the fulness of time he came into the world, and was made flesh, and God and man being as truly united in one person, as the reasonable soul and flesh is one man. This adorable person lived, and suffered, and died, as the representative of his people. The righteousness of his life was to be their right and title to life, and the righteousness of his sufferings and death was to save them from all the sufferings due to their sins. And thus the law and justice of the Father would be glorified in pardoning them, and his faithfulness and holiness made honourable in saving them. He might be strictly just, and yet the justifier of him who believeth in Jesus.

In this covenant the Holy Spirit, a person co-equal and co-eternal with the Father and the Son, undertook the gracious office of quickening and convincing sinners in their consciences, how guilty they were, and how much they wanted a Saviour, and in their judgments how able he was to save all that come unto God through him, and in their hearts to receive him, and to believe unto righteousness, and then in their walk and conversation to live upon his grace and strength. His office is thus described by our blessed Lord in John xvi. 13, 14:—
" When the Spirit of truth is come, he shall glorify me; for he shall take of mine, and shall show it unto you;" that is, when he comes to convince sinners of sin, and of righteousness, and of judgment, he takes of the things of Christ, and glorifies him by showing them what a

fulness there is in him to save. He leads them into all necessary truth in their judgments, both concerning their own sinfulness, guilt, and helplessness, and also concerning the almighty power of the God-man, and his lawful authority to make use of it for their salvation. He opens their understandings to comprehend the covenant of grace, and the offices of the eternal Trinity in this covenant, particularly the office of the sinner's surety, the Lord Christ; and he convinces them that there is righteousness and strength, comfort and rejoicing, grace for grace, holiness and glory, yea, treasures infinite, everlasting treasures of these in Christ; and hereby he draws out their affections after Christ, and enables them with the heart to believe in him unto righteousness. And the Holy Spirit having thus brought them to the happy knowledge of their union with Christ, afterwards glorifies him in their walk and conversation, by teaching them how to live by faith upon his fulness, and to be continually receiving out of it grace for grace, according to their continual needs.

The corruption of our nature by the fall, and our recovery through Jesus Christ, are the two leading truths in the Christian religion; and I suppose the persons for whose sake this little tract is drawn up not only to know them, but also to be established in them, steadfastly to believe and deeply to experience them. The necessity of their being well grounded in them is very evident; for a sinner will never seek after nor desire Christ, farther than he feels his guilt and his misery; nor will he receive Christ by faith, till all other methods of saving himself fail; nor will he live upon Christ's fulness farther than he has an abiding sense of his own want of him. Reader, how do these truths appear to thee? Has the law of God arraigned thee in thy conscience? Hast thou been there brought in guilty, and has the Spirit of God deeply convinced thee by the law of sin, and of unbelief, and of thy helplessness, so as to leave thee no false resting-place short of Christ? Has he swept away every refuge of lies; and thus put thee upon inquiring what thou must do to be saved? If not, may the Lord the Spirit convince thee, and in his own good time bring thee to the knowledge of thyself, and to the saving knowledge of and belief in Christ Jesus, without which this book can profit thee nothing. But if thou hast been thus convinced, and the Lord has shone into thy understanding, and enlightened it with the knowledge of the way of salvation, then read on. May the Lord make what thou readest profitable to thine establishment in the faith, which is in Christ Jesus!

There are two things spoken of faith in Scripture, which highly deserve the attention of every true believer. The first is the state of safety, in which he is placed by Christ, and is delivered from every evil and danger in time and in eternity, to which sin had justly exposed him; and the second is the happiness of this state, consisting in an abundant supply of all spiritual blessings freely given to him in Christ, and received, as they are wanted, by the hand of faith out of the fulness of Christ. By which means, whoever has obtained this precious faith ought to have a quiet conscience at peace with God, and need not fear any manner of evil, how much soever it be deserved; and thereby he may at all times come boldly to the throne of grace, to receive whatever is necessary for his comfortable walk heavenwards. Every grace, every blessing promised in Scripture, is his, and he may and does enjoy them so far as he lives by faith upon the Son of God; so far his life and conversation are well ordered, his walk is even, his spiritual enemies are conquered, the old man is mortified with his affections and lusts, and the new man is renewed day by day after the image of God in righteousness and true holiness. And from what he already enjoys by faith, and from the hopes of a speedy and perfect enjoyment, the Scripture warrants him to rejoice in the Lord with joy unspeakable and full of glory.

It is much to be lamented, that few live up to these two privileges of faith. Many persons, who are truly concerned about the salvation of their souls, live for years together full of doubts and fears, and are not established in the faith that is in Christ Jesus; and several who are in a good measure established, yet do not walk happily in an even course, nor experience the continual blessedness of receiving by faith a supply of every want out of the Saviour's fulness. These things I have long observed, and what I have been taught of them from the Scripture, and from the good hand of God upon me, I have put together, and throw it as a mite into the treasury. I am sure it was never more wanted than at present. May the good Lord accept the poor offering, and bless it to the hearts of his dear people, to the praise of the glory of his own grace!

For the clearer understanding of what shall be spoken upon the Life of Faith, it will be needful to consider first what faith is; for a man must have faith before he can make use of it. He must be in Christ, before he can live upon Christ. Now faith signifies the believing the truth of the word of God: so says Christ, "Thy word is truth:" it relates to some word spoken, or to some promise made by him, and it expresses the belief which a person who hears it has of its being true. He assents to it, relies upon it, and acts accordingly. This is faith. And the whole word of God, which is the ground of faith, may be reduced to two points; namely, to what the law reveals concerning the justification of a righteous man, and to what the gospel reveals concerning the salvation of a sinner. A short examination of these points will discover to us a great number of persons, who have no faith at all in the word of God.

First.—Every man in his natural state, before the grace of Christ, and the inspiration of his Spirit, has no faith. The Scripture says, God hath shut up all that are in this state in unbelief; and when the Holy Spirit awakens any one of them, he convinces him of sin, and of unbelief in particular. "When the Comforter is come," says Christ, "he shall convince the world of sin, because they believe not in me."

Secondly.—A man who lives careless in sin has no faith. He does not believe one word that God says in his law. Let it warn him of his guilt, and show him his great danger, yet he sets at nought the terrors of the Lord. He acts as if there was no day of judgment, and no place of eternal torments. He has no fear of God before his eyes. How can such a practical atheist as this have any faith?

Thirdly.—The formalist has not true faith. He is content with the form of godliness, and denies the power of it. The veil of unbelief is upon his heart, and the pride of his own good works and duties is ever before his eyes, that he finds no want of the salvation of Jesus, and is averse to the grace of the gospel. All his hopes arise from what he is in himself, and from what he is able to do for himself. He neither believes God speaking in the law, nor in the gospel. If he believed his word in the law, it would convict him of sin, and forbid him to go about to establish a righteousness of his own; because by the works of the law shall no flesh living be justified; yet this he does not believe. If he believed the word of God in the gospel, it would convince him of righteousness, of an infinitely perfect righteousness, wrought out by the God-man Christ Jesus, and imputed to the sinner without any works of his own: for unto him that worketh not, but believeth on him that justifieth the ungodly, his faith is imputed for righteousness. To this he dare not trust wholly for his acceptance before God; therefore he has not true faith.

Fourthly.—A man may be so far enlightened, as to understand the way of salvation, and yet have not true faith. This is a possible case. The apostle states it, 1 Cor. xiii. 2, "Though I understand all mysteries, and all knowledge, yet I may be nothing." And it is a dangerous case, as Heb. x. 26, "If we sin wilfully after that we have received the knowledge of the truth, there remaineth no more sacrifice for sins." Here was such a knowledge of the truth, as left a man to perish without the benefit of Christ's sacrifice; therefore he wanted that faith, which whosoever hath shall be saved.

What great numbers are there under these delusions! Reader, art thou one of them? Examine closely: for it is of eternal moment. Prove thine own self, whether thou be in the faith. If thou askest how thou shalt know it, since there are so many errors about it; hear what God's word says,—Whoever believes truly, has been first convinced of unbelief. This our Lord teaches, John xvi. 9, "When the Comforter is come, he will convince the world of sin, because they believe not on me." He convinces of sin, by enlightening the understanding to know the exceeding sinfulness of it: and by quickening the conscience to feel the guilt of it. He shows the misery threatened, and leaves sinners no false refuge to flee unto. He will not suffer them to sit down content with some sorrow, or a little outward reformation, or any supposed righteousness, but makes them feel that, do whatever they will or can, still their guilt remains. Thus he puts them upon seeking out for salvation, and by the gospel he discovers it to them. He opens their understandings to know what they hear and read concerning the covenant of the eternal Trinity, and concerning what the God-man has done in the fulfilling of this covenant.

The Holy Spirit teaches them the nature of the adorable person of Christ-God manifest in the flesh, and the infinitely precious and everlasting meritorious righteousness, which he has wrought out by the obedience of his life and death; and he convinces them, that this righteousness is sufficient for their salvation, and that nothing is required except faith, for its being imputed unto them; and he works in them a sense of their being helpless and without strength to rely upon this righteousness, and through faith in it to have peace with God. He makes them see, that they cannot by any power of their own in the least depend upon it; for all their sufficiency is of God. It requires the same arm of the Lord, which wrought out this righteousness, to enable them with the heart to believe in it. They are made clearly sensible of this from the word and Spirit of God, and from their own daily experience; and thereby they are disposed to receive their whole salvation from the free grace of God, and to him to ascribe all the glory of it. These are the redeemed of the Lord, to whom it is given to believe. They are quickened from a death in trespasses and sins, their consciences are awakened, their understandings are enlightened with the knowledge of Christ, they are enabled in their wills to choose him, and in their hearts to love him, and to rejoice in his salvation. This is entirely the work of the Holy Spirit; for faith is his gift. (Eph. ii. 8.) Unto you it is given, says the apostle (Phil. i. 29), in the behalf of Christ to believe on him; none can give it but the Spirit of God; because it is the faith of the operation of God, and requires the same almighty power to believe with the heart, as it did to raise Christ's body from the grave. (Eph. i. 20.) And this power he puts forth in the preaching of the word, and makes it the power of God unto salvation. The word is called (2 Cor. iii. 8) the ministration of the Spirit, because by it the Spirit ministers his grace and strength. So Gal. iii. 2, "Received ye the Spirit by the works of the law, or by the hearing of faith?" It was by hearing faith preached, that they received the Spirit; for faith cometh by hearing, and hearing by the word of God, which is therefore called the word of faith. And thus the word is the means, in the hand of the Spirit, to dispose the hearts of those who hear it to receive and to embrace Christ; whereby they attain the righteousness of faith, as Rom. x. 10: "With the heart man believeth unto righteousness." The heart is the chief thing in believing; for into it Christ is received, and in it he dwells by faith. The vital union between Christ and the believer is manifested and made known in the heart, and therein it is cemented and established. With joy can the believer say, "My beloved is mine, and I am his;" happy for me, we are but one person in the eye of the law, and our interests are but one. Blessed state this! Christ gives himself freely to the believer, who also gives himself up in faith to Christ. Christ, as the believer's surety, has taken his sins upon himself, and the believer takes Christ's righteousness; for Christ makes over all that he has to the believer, who by faith looks upon it, and makes use of it, as his own; according to that express warrant for his so doing in 1 Cor. iii. 22, 23:—All things are yours, because ye belong to Christ.

This vital union, between Christ and the believer, is

largely treated of in Scripture. Christ thus speaks of it in his prayer for his people (John xvii.) :—" I pray for them who shall believe on me, through their word; that they all may be one, as thou Father art in me, and I in thee; that they also may be one in us. I in them, and thou in me, that they may be made perfect in one." And in John vi. 56, he says, "He that eateth my flesh, and drinketh my blood, dwelleth in me and I in him;" and this indwelling is by faith, as Eph. iii. 17: "That Christ may dwell in your hearts by faith." And it is the office of the Holy Spirit to manifest this union to their hearts, as John xiv. 20: "At that day, when the Spirit of truth is come, ye shall know that I am in my Father, and you in me, and I in you." And besides these, and many other plain words, this union is also represented by several striking images, such as that of husband and wife, who are in law but one person, the husband being answerable for the wife's debts, and the wife sharing in her husband's honours and goods. It is set forth by the union between a building and the foundation upon which it stands secure; between a tree and its branches, which live because they are in the tree, and grow by the sap which they receive from it; between the head and the members, which by holding under the head, live and grow, having a supply of nourishment administered to every part. Under these beautiful images, the Scripture sets forth the reality and the blessed fruits of this union. The Holy Spirit makes it known to the believer, by enabling him to rely on God's word as infallible truth, and to receive Christ's person as the Almighty Saviour; and he strengthens it by enabling the believer to make use of Christ's fulness, and to live by faith upon him in all his offices, for the partaking of all his promised graces and blessings. That faith, which is of the operation of God, always produces the knowledge and the fruits of this blessed union,.and enables the soul to give itself up to Christ, that it may be one with him, not in a figurative, metaphorical way, but as really and truly as the building is one with the foundation; as much one in interest as husband and wife; one in influence, as the root and the branches, the head and the members. So that this is not an empty notion about Christ, or some clear knowledge of him, or a mere approving of his way of salvation, but it is an actual receiving of him into the heart for righteousness to justify, and to dwell and reign there to sanctify; a receiving him as a perfect Saviour, and living upon him and his fulness; waiting upon him to be taught daily; trusting wholly for acceptance to his blood and righteousness; resting, relying, leaning upon his promised strength to hold out unto the end; and hoping for eternal life as the free gift of God through Jesus Christ our Lord. The saving faith thus receives Christ, and thus lives upon Christ. Now, reader, examine and prove thyself whether thou hast this faith. Dost thou believe with thy heart unto righteousness? Thou canst not live upon Christ unless thou art first in Christ. Thou must be first persuaded of thine interest in him, before thou canst make use of it and improve it; and therefore the knowledge of thy union with him must be clear and plain before thou canst have a free and open communion with him. There must be faith before there can be the fruits of faith, and strong faith before there can be much and ripe fruit. Little faith will receive but little from Christ. The weak believer is full of doubts and fears; and when he wants comfort or strength, or any other things which Christ has promised to give his people, he is questioning whether he has any right to expect them; and therefore he does not receive them, because he has not boldness and access with confidence to God by faith in Christ Jesus. From hence appears the necessity of being established in the faith. The believer must have clear evidence of his interest in Christ before he can live comfortable and happy upon Christ; therefore he must look well to the foundation, and see there be no doubts left about his being settled upon it. Christ being the sure foundation, how can he safely build thereon all his salvation, unless he be first satisfied that he is upon it? The peace with God in his conscience, every act of spiritual life, and the whole walk and well ordering of his conversation, depend upon the settling of this point.

It ought to be finally determined and brought to this issue—"Christ is mine; I know it from the word of God. I have the witness of the Spirit of God; and Christ allows me, unworthy as I am, to make use of him and of his fulness for the supply of all my needs; and I find I do make use of him, and thereby I know from daily experience that I am in him, because I live upon him." According as this point is settled, so in proportion will be the life of faith. If the believer be thoroughly grounded in it, without any doubt or fear, then he may and will with confidence improve his interest in Christ; but if he still leave it in suspense, his faith can be but little, and therefore he will obtain little comfort or strength from Christ.

Reader, art thou one of the weak in faith? Dost thou feel it? Dost thou mourn for it? And dost thou know from whence thy faith is to be strengthened? Who can increase it but he alone who gives it? O pray, then, to the Lord God to give thee the spirit of wisdom and revelation, that the eyes of thy understanding may be enlightened to see the infinite sufficiency of Christ's person, as God-man, and the everlasting merit of his life and death to save his people from their sins. And whatever hinders thee from seeing the fulness of Christ's salvation, and resting comfortably by faith upon it, earnestly entreat the Lord to remove it. If it be sin, beg of God to make thee more willing to part with it. If it be guilt, pray him to ordain peace in thy conscience, through the blood of sprinkling. If it be much corruption, it cannot be subdued until it be first pardoned. If thou hast got under the spirit of bondage, look up to the Lord Christ for that liberty wherewith he makes his people free. Whatever it be, as soon as it is discovered to thee, make use of prayer, believing God's word of faithfulness, that what thou askest thou shalt have, and that he will so establish thee that thou shalt go on from faith to faith. May it be thy happy case! Amen.

Reader, if thou art an awakened man, convinced of sin by the word and Spirit of God, all thine enemies will try to keep thee from the clear knowledge of thy union with

Christ. The reason is plain, because then thou wilt not be able to depend upon Christ's promised strength, and to make use of it by faith, which is almighty to defeat them all. Hearken not, therefore, to any suggestion, nor be afraid of any opposition, which would hinder thee from seeking to be fully convinced of thine interest in Christ, and of thy being a branch in the true vine. Satan will use all his wiles and fiery darts, and all carnal professors will be on his side, and they will have close allies in thine own breast, in thine unbelief, in thy legal spirit, and in thy lusts and corruptions. Consider why do these enemies fight so hard against thy being safely settled and comfortably grounded upon Christ by living faith? Is it not because thou wilt then be an overmatch for them, through the strength of Jesus? And does not this plainly show thee the absolute necessity of knowing that Christ and thou are one? Till this be known, thou wilt be afraid to apply to him, and to make use of his strength; and till thou dost use it, all thine enemies will triumph over thee. O beg of God, then, to increase thy faith, that thou mayest be fully convinced of thy union with Christ, and mayest live in him safe, and on him happy. Hear and read his word, and pray for the effectual working of the Lord the Spirit in it and by it, that faith may come and grow by hearing, until it be finally settled, without doubt or wavering, that Christ is thine and thou art his. After the believer is thus grounded and established in the knowledge of his union with Christ, it behoves him then to inquire what God has given him a right to in consequence of this union; and the Scripture will inform him, that in the covenant of grace it has pleased the Father that all fulness should dwell in his Son, as the head, for the use of his members. He has it to supply all their need. They cannot possibly want anything, but it is treasured up for them in his infinite fulness; there they may have it, grace for grace, every moment as their occasions require; and they have it in no other way, and by no other hand than faith, trusting the word of promise, and relying upon Christ's faithfulness and power to fulfil it: as it is written, "the just shall live by his faith." (Hab. ii. 4.) Having received justification to life by faith in the righteousness of Christ, he depends on Christ to keep him alive, and makes use of Christ's fulness for all the wants of that spiritual life which he has given. He trusts him for them all, and lives upon him by faith for the continual receiving of them all; and according to his faith so it is done unto him.

Let this be well weighed and considered, that the justified person lives and performs every act of spiritual life by faith. This is a very important lesson, and therefore it is taught in Scripture as plainly as words can speak. Everything is promised to, and is received by faith. Thus it is said, Ye are all the children of God by faith in Christ Jesus; and if children, then heirs according to the promise, heirs of God and joint heirs with Christ, who of God is made unto us wisdom, righteousness, and holiness, made for their use, wisdom to teach them, righteousness to justify them, and holiness to sanctify them; yea, he has all things in his fulness for their use, as the free grant speaks (1 Cor. iii. 21), &c.: "All things are yours, whether Paul or Apollos, or Cephas, or the world, or life, or death, or things present, or things to come; all are yours, and ye are Christ's, and Christ is God's." Consider, believer, what a large estate this is: thy title to it is good, and thou enterest into possession by faith. See then that thou make use of thine inheritance, and live upon it. Do not say, when thou wantest anything, I know not where to get it; for whatever the God-man has of wisdom, righteousness, holiness, power, and glory, he has it, as the head of the body, for thee as one of his members, for thy use and benefit; and he has promised it to thee in his word. Make free with him then. Go to him with confidence. Thou canst not do him greater honour than to receive from him what he has to give. That is glorifying him. It is putting the crown upon his head, and confessing him to be a perfect, all-sufficient Christ when it pleaseth thee, as it did his Father, that in him should all fulness dwell, and when thou art content to live out of thyself upon his fulness for the supply of all thy needs in time and in eternity. To live thus upon him is his glory, and it is thy privilege, thy interest, and thy happiness. In every state, spiritual and temporal, and in every circumstance thou canst possibly be in, thou art commanded to look up to Christ, that thou mayest receive out of his fulness, and to depend upon him to save thee from every evil, and to bestow upon thee every good. In thy walk heavenwards, and in everything thou meetest with by the way, put thy trust in Christ, and expect from him the fulfilling of all his promises. He has all power in heaven and earth, for that very purpose. Still rely upon him, and cast thy burdens on him, when thou art tempted; when old corruptions arise, when the world and the devil assault thee, when under a sense of weakness and dulness in duty, when in darkness and desertion, in persecution and trouble, in pain and poverty, in sickness and death. This is the Life of Faith. Thou wilt live like a Christian indeed, if, being in any of these cases, thou believest that Christ is able, because he is almighty, and willing, because he has promised, to supply thy wants, and then canst trust in him for that supply. Depend upon it, thou shalt have it, and it shall be done unto thee according to his word.

After the believer is become one with Christ, and through him has a right to all the riches of grace, and may by faith make use of them as his own, why is he so long in learning this lesson perfectly? Being adopted into the heavenly family, and an heir of the heavenly inheritance, why does not he immediately live up to his privilege, and to his estate? His title is good. The inheritance is sure. All things are become his: for all fulness is in Christ, and by virtue of his union with Christ, this fulness is his: and he may by faith be always receiving out of it every grace and blessing, which Christ has promised: why then does not he at once attain to this happy Life of Faith? Sad experience proves that young believers do not. They meet with so many difficulties, that they grow up slowly into Christ in all things. They do not attain to a solid establishment in the faith in a day. Enemies without and within stop their progress, insomuch that they often continue little children for a long time. They have the same right to Christ, the same privileges, and the same promised grace, which young men and fathers in Christ have, but they have not learned by experience how to improve their interest in him, and to make the most of it. The difficulties and temptations which weaken their hold of Christ, and stop their growth in him, are many; some of the chief are these:—

1. They continue little children and weak in faith, because they do not presently attain a solid acquaintance with the person of Christ, and are not thoroughly satisfied, how able he was and sufficient for everything he undertook, and how perfectly he has finished every part of his work.

2. This keeps them ignorant of many things in which the glory of his salvation consists; hence they have not clear believing views of its fulness and of its freeness.

3. By which means they labour under many doubts about the manner of their receiving this salvation. A legal spirit working with their unbelief puts them upon reasoning continually against being saved freely by grace through faith; and—

4. These legal unbelieving reasonings gain great power from their unskilfulness in their warfare between nature and grace, the old man and the new, the flesh and the spirit; and—

5. All these difficulties are mightily strengthened from their hearkening to sense, and trusting to its reports more than to the word of God. While believers are under these difficulties, their faith meets with many checks in its growth, and until they be enabled to overcome them, they continue to be little children in Christ. Their weak faith receives but little from Christ, and it continues weak, because they have but little dependence upon the effectual working of Christ's mighty power. The exceeding greatness of his power is able to strengthen them, and he has promised it, but they dare not trust

him. Consider, therefore, reader, if thou art one of these babes, why thou dost not grow up faster into Christ.

The first thing that stops thee is the ignorance which is in thy mind about his person, and the prejudice against him, which is in thy carnal heart. These are in all men by nature; and these Satan will work upon, in order to hinder the increase of thy faith. He will use all his cunning, and his power, to keep thee from growing in that knowledge of Christ which is eternal life. He will inject into thy heart blasphemous thoughts against his Godhead; and when thou art reading in Scripture, or hearing about his being God manifest in the flesh, he will try to puzzle and perplex thy imagination with a How can these things be? He will represent the union of the two natures in Christ as a thing not to be understood, and as if they who believed it with the clearest evidence of God's word and Spirit, had only some fancy about it. He has an old grudge against Christ, and will not scruple to tell any lies of him. He was a liar from the beginning, and abode not in the truth. Regard him not. Mind what the word of truth says, and pray thou mayest understand it: for the more thou knowest of the Lord Christ, that blessed God-man, the more wilt thou be settled and established in him. It is written of him, first, that he is God, true and very God, in the holy, blessed, and glorious Trinity; a person co-equal and co-eternal with the Father and the Holy Spirit (Isa. ix. 6): "Unto us a child is born, who is the mighty God." Secondly, that he is Jehovah, which signifies the self-existent essence (Isa. xliii. 11): "I, even I, am Jehovah, and besides me there is no Saviour." From whence it is evident, that the Saviour is Jehovah, and that he exists in a manner independent of, and distinct from, all other beings and things. St. Jude makes the opposition to this fundamental truth the condemning sin of certain heretics, who denied Jesus Christ to be the only Lord God and our Lord. In the covenant of grace this divine person undertook to be made man. He who was true and very God was made true and very man; he had a reasonable soul and human flesh, and was in all points like other men, sin excepted. And as the reasonable soul and flesh is one man, so God and man is one Christ. This is the glorious person who undertook in the covenant of grace to be man's surety. St. Paul calls him the surety of the New Testament; and what could there be wanting in him for this high office? He is every way qualified to be the surety for man, who is himself true and very man; who is also God as well as man, and therefore has all the perfections of Jehovah to render what he did and suffered as man's surety infinitely and everlastingly meritorious. This is the blessed object of faith, God and man united in one Christ. Consider, then, reader, what the Scripture says of his wonderful person, in order that thy faith in him may be established. That very self-existent God, who spake and all things were made, who commanded and they stand fast to this very hour, was made flesh. He came to be the surety for his people, to obey and suffer in their stead. What could not his almighty power effect? Is anything too hard for the Lord God? What obedience can his Father's law demand, which he is not infinitely able to pay? What sufferings can satisfy his Father's justice, which he is not absolutely qualified to endure? For he has every perfection and attribute equal with the Father. On this truth thou must rest; and is it not a sure foundation? In the certainty of it thou must seek to be more grounded every day: because as thou growest in the knowledge of his divine person, thou wilt become more satisfied of his infinite sufficiency to save; and fully convinced of this, thou wilt be enabled from Scripture to answer and silence thine own unbelieving thoughts, and to reject the blasphemous suggestions of Satan against the Lord Christ. Observe, then, that he is God, and that he is Jehovah. Read and meditate on what the Scripture says of his Godhead, and pray that thou mayest be taught of God to understand it; for no man can say that Jesus is the Lord but by the Holy Ghost. It is his office to glorify Jesus, by enabling thee to believe him to be Lord and God, and to call him thy Lord and thy God;

and to prove he is so, by thy humble dependence upon him for every blessing, both in time and in eternity.

It is much to be lamented, that believers in general take so little pains to get a clear knowledge of the doctrine of the ever-blessed Trinity; for want of which their faith is unsettled, and they are liable to many errors both in judgment and in practice. I would therefore most earnestly recommend it to all that are weak in faith, to be diligent in hearing and reading what in Scripture is revealed concerning the Trinity in Unity, looking up always for the inward teaching of the Holy Spirit; and I would direct them to a form of sound words in the Common Prayer-book for Trinity Sunday, which contains the shortest and best account of the subject that I ever saw. "It is very meet, right, and our bounden duty, that we should at all times, and in all places, give thanks unto thee, O Lord, almighty, everlasting God; who art one God, one Lord, not one only person, but three persons in one substance: for that which we believe of the glory of the Father, the same we believe of the Son, and of the Holy Ghost, without any difference or inequality." These are precious words. Meditate, reader, upon them, and entreat the Holy Spirit to enlighten thine understanding with the saving knowledge of them, that being established in the doctrine of the ever-blessed Trinity, and of the Godhead of the Lord Christ, thou mayest be enabled to overcome the difficulties which arose,

Secondly,—From thy not being well acquainted with the nature of Christ's salvation, concerning which young believers are apt to have many doubts. Carnal reason is strong in them. The spirit of bondage resists with many and mighty arguments, and unbelief musters up all its forces, and there is a long and obstinate fight against being saved freely and fully by the grace of Christ Jesus. But the arguments which God has provided in his word, when applied by his Spirit, will prevail and overcome. Meditate upon them for the establishing of thy weak faith. Consider, first, the covenant. Salvation is not a thing of chance, or left to man's will or power, but it wa contrived by the blessed Trinity in the covenant of grace, and everything belonging to it was perfectly settled. It is said to be (2 Sam. xxiii. 5) an everlasting covenant, ordered in all things, and sure. O thou of little faith, why then dost thou doubt? What! doubt of God's love? Here is a covenant springing from his mere love, and from everlasting. Doubt of its being well contrived? Infinite wisdom orders it in all things. Doubt of its being well executed? It is in all things sure, sure as God's almighty power and faithfulness can make it. What motives are here for the strengthening of thy faith? May the Lord render them effectual! Reflect, secondly, upon the undertakings of the Lord Christ, the surety of this covenant. There was nothing left out of this covenant: it was ordered in all things belonging to salvation, and Christ undertook to perform all things on the part of his Father, that his law might be magnified, and his justice made honourable and glorious; and on the part of the sinner, that he might be saved from all evil, and entitled to all good. And being God and man united in one Christ, he was a proper surety to reconcile God to man, and to reconcile man to God. May these things, then, sink deep into thy heart, that thy surety has undertaken the whole of thy salvation, to do all for thee, and all in thee, and all by thee. What canst thou desire more for the settling of thy faith?

Thirdly.—Perhaps thou wilt say, his undertakings were great, but has he fulfilled them? Yes, and so perfectly, that he is able to save to the uttermost. He was called Jesus, because he was to save his people from their sins; as their surety, he was to fulfil the law for them by his obedience, and to suffer the pains and penalties of it by his death and passion. Accordingly, in the fulness of time he was manifest in the flesh, and came to do the will of his Father: of his obedience to that will he thus speaks: "I have finished the work which thou gavest me to do." Of his suffering that will, he said, with his last breath, "It is finished." Observe, whatever he undertook to do in his life and death was finished; and it was demonstrated that, as man's surety, he had done and suffered everything ordered in the covenant, by his resurrection from the dead: for then did the Father declare him to be the Son of God with power. Will not all this satisfy thee, O thou of little faith? Here is one more cause of thy doubting removed; thou canst not deny but Christ has finished everything he undertook, and in consequence thereof he has all power in heaven and earth to bestow a full and finished salvation. What canst thou now object?

Fourthly.—Does a thought arise in thy heart? It is finished: but is it so freely given, that such an unworthy creature as I am may partake of it? Yes: it comes to thee in the way of a free gift. Great, inestimable, and eternal, as it is, yet it is all thine in receiving. Not he who worketh, but he who believeth, is justified from all things. It is by faith that believers are justified and sanctified, are strengthened and comforted in their walk; by faith they fight against all their enemies, and by faith they conquer and lay hold of eternal life. And therefore it is all of faith, that it might be by grace. Salvation is wrought out and finished by thy surety, given to thee freely, continued with all its blessings in time and through eternity, as a free gift, to the praise of the glory of free grace. Why, therefore, art thou discouraged? Hast thou nothing to buy with? Then obey the Lord's command. Come and buy free salvation, without money and without price. How should this motive still add to the establishment of thy faith! for there thou seest whatever thou wantest is thine by believing. Thou mayest have it freely by grace. It is treasured up for thee in the fulness of thy dear Saviour, and thou canst not honour him more than to make free use of it. What dost thou say to this? Hast thou anything to object? Canst thou find any fault with the covenant of grace, or with the undertakings of the God-man in it? No, certainly, the covenant was well ordered in all things and sure, and what the surety of the covenant undertook he has perfectly fulfilled. Salvation is finished on his part; he has glorified the law by his infinitely perfect obedience; he has made divine justice honourable by his sufferings and death; he has brought in everlasting righteousness for his people, and will bring them to everlasting glory; for he has already taken possession of it for them as the head of the body the church, and he has all power in heaven and earth to save them day by day, until he make them partakers of his eternal salvation. What can thy heart wish for more, than such a Saviour, and such a salvation? O! be not faithless then, but believing; and if thou hast any doubts left, endeavour to have them cleared up by reading and prayer, until thy faith be perfectly settled on the divinity of God thy Saviour, and the infinite sufficiency of his salvation. These two points lie at the very foundation of the Christian religion: they must be supposed in all its principles, and built upon in all its practice; therefore, being of universal influence, if they be thoroughly established, thy faith will be steadfast, and thy life well ordered and comfortable. Examine, then, and prove thyself here, before thou readest any farther. Dost thou believe Christ to be true and very God, in every perfection and attribute equal with the Father? And is his a full and a free salvation? All the following directions depend upon, and can only profit thee, so far as thou believest these two points. Look well, then, to thy establishment in them. If it be strong, the life of faith will be steady and prosperous; but if it be weak, thou wilt be liable to be tossed about continually with errors, and overcome with temptations, especially with those to which a legal spirit will expose thee, as I purposed to show under the

Third general head, in which is to be considered how the little children in Christ, for want of being established in the belief of his Godhead, and of his full and free salvation, labour under many doubts: a legal spirit working with their unbelief puts them upon reasoning continually against being saved freely by grace through faith.

He is of a legal spirit who is under the law, and apprehends himself bound to keep it as the condition of life, requiring of him, Do this and thou shalt live. In his understanding he sees this and no other way to life; in his will he is continually inclined to it, and in his heart he loves it, because he fancies it in his own power to attain life in this way, and he can merit it by his own works, which mightily gratifies his self-love and indulges his pride. This legal spirit reigns over all men in their natural state, but does not discover its tyranny until it be opposed; and then so soon as the soul is quickened from a death in trespasses and sins, it begins to fight, trying to keep the poor sinner in bondage by its legal workings and strivings, and putting him upon seeking for some good disposition or qualification in himself, on account of which God should love him. Thus the awakened soul, under the spirit of bondage, always seeks deliverance by the works of that law, which can do nothing more than bring him to the knowledge of sin, discover to him the exceeding sinfulness of it, and the exceeding great punishment which it deserves; by which means it is always nourishing the doubts and fears of unbelief. And after the Lord has in a measure removed them by a clear discovery of the salvation that is in Jesus, and by the gift of faith, yet still this legal spirit will be trying to bring the soul into bondage again to fear; and it too often prevails. Young believers find it the worst enemy they have to deal with. It is a sly, subtle foe, that seems to intend them a kindness, while it is always on the side of their greatest enemy. It would appear to them to be actuated by a zeal for God, but it is to eclipse the glory of the Lord Christ, to take away the all-sufficiency of his salvation, and to rob them of their great joy and peace in believing. If any one should ask how this legal spirit comes to have such power over mankind, the Scripture informs us,

First,—That all men, being God's creatures, are under the law to him, bound to keep it; or bound, if they transgress, to suffer the threatened pains and penalties. In this state man was created, and in it all men are by nature; and therefore there is in us all a continual leaning to the law, and a desire to attain righteousness by the works of it. We are all wedded to this way of gaining God's favour. The apostle says there is a marriage union between us and the law; and it, like a husband, has dominion over us as long as it liveth; so that we cannot be married to Christ until that be dead wherein we were held. You may see this in the Jews. How does Moses labour to bring them off from an opinion of their own righteousness? And a greater than Moses has done the same in his discourses against the Scribes and Pharisees: yea, the apostles of our Lord were forced to write and preach against this leaning to the law, it gave such disturbance to the true disciples of Christ. And notwithstanding the Scripture arguments against it, yet we have great numbers among us who seek for a justifying righteousness by the works of the law. And they are put upon seeking this,

Secondly,—From their ignorance of the law. They are not acquainted with its nature, for it demands what they cannot pay. It insists upon an obedience, spiritual, perfect, and uninterrupted; for the least offence, if but in thought, it comes with its fearful sentence, "*Cursed is every one who continueth not in all things that are written in the book of the law to do them.*" On him who does not continue in all things,—and not one man ever did,—this sentence takes place; and if he was to live a thousand years, he could not do anything to repeal it. The law will always be to him the ministration of condemnation and the ministration of death; and that is all it can do for him. It provides no remedy, and gives him no hope, but leaves him condemned to the first and to the second death; and yet such is the blindness of the sinner, that he will be still leaning to the law, and afraid to trust wholly to the righteousness of Christ; and this arises,

Thirdly,—From his ignorance of Christ's righteousness, which is infinitely perfect, and wants no works of the law to be joined with it in the justifying of a sinner; because it is the righteousness of God, wrought out by the God-man for his people, and it is the righteousness of faith. They receive it by faith, without works, so that it is directly opposite to the righteousness of a legal spirit. Hence we have many among us, great professors too, who are ignorant of God's righteousness; they have not been entirely brought off from a legal bottom, and therefore they talk of being justified without a justifying righteousness; which if God was to do, he would be unrighteous, and which, as he has declared he will not do, their fancied justification leaves them still in their sins. They dare not put their whole trust and confidence in the righteousness of Christ imputed unto sinners, and made theirs by faith. They have many fears about imputed righteousness, although the apostle has not scrupled to mention it eleven times in one chapter (Rom. iv.); and these fears make them read the Scripture with such prejudice, that they say they cannot find the expression, *faith in the righteousness of Christ*, in all the Bible. They may find the sense of the expression in Moses, and in all the prophets, and the very words in 2 Peter i. 1:—"Simon Peter, a servant and an apostle of Jesus Christ, to them who have obtained like precious faith with us in [the Greek is $\varepsilon\iota\varsigma$] the righteousness of God, and our Saviour Jesus Christ." Here is faith in the righteousness of Christ, with several glorious titles to recommend it; namely it is the righteousness of God, of God our Saviour, of Jesus Christ. From whence can men's opposition to this way of justification arise, but from their not being convinced by the Spirit of God of the necessity of Christ's righteousness? It is his peculiar office to convince us of this truth. No teaching but his can do it. O that he may do it in the hearts of those who, out of a zeal for God, though not according to knowledge, eclipse the glory of the Lord, and rob afflicted consciences of their comfort by opposing imputed righteousness! It is a righteousness of so high and heavenly a nature, wrought out by another, and so wonderful a person, is bestowed as a free gift upon the chief of sinners, whereby alone they obtain remission of their sins, and are made partakers of the kingdom of heaven; and they receive it by faith only, without works, which a legal spirit always wants to mix with it, that no one could ever believe in it unless it were given him from above. May it be given to those professors who cannot yet submit to the righteousness of Christ, to see their want of it, and with the heart to believe in it unto salvation! Reader, hast thou not found what an enemy this legal spirit is to thy peace and joy, and how it is always inclining thee to some self-righteousness, through thy ignorance of the righteousness of the law and of the righteousness of faith? And wouldst thou gladly be delivered from it? Know, then, that nothing can subdue it but the bringing into thy conscience a better hope, from a better righteousness than that of the law; and when thou art enabled to plead it there, against all the charges of sin and Satan, then thou wilt stand fast in the liberty wherewith Christ hath made thee free. His is a better righteousness; it is infinitely perfect and everlasting, even the righteousness of God; by faith in this righteousness thou shalt be saved from the law, and shalt receive remission of sins; through it the Father doth accept thee, and give thee the Spirit of his Son to lead, and comfort, and sanctify thee; he doth love thee and bless thee, as his dear child, making all things work together under him for thy good, and keeping thee by his mighty power through faith unto salvation; so that in and on account of this righteousness thou shalt be saved from all the evils of sin, and receive all spiritual blessings in earth and heaven. And this thou shalt have freely, without any merit or work of the law; for this righteousness comes wholly by grace, and is for thee a sinner as such, and is to justify thee from the condemnation of the law, to turn its curses into blessings, and its threatened punishments into happiness. And this it can do for thee perfectly and everlastingly; so that being found in this righteousness, there is no grace promised in time, or glory in eternity, but it shall be thine. The Lord God promises them to thee, in the fullest and freest manner,—to thee, without any exception or limitation, being a sinner and ungodly; though one of the vilest and basest, yet to thee, as such, is the word of this salvation sent. And it will be all thine in the comfortable enjoyment of it, through believing. Thou art to bring nothing to recommend thee, but that thou art a sensible sinner, and thy right and title to a finished salvation is clear from the warrant of God's word, when thou believest with thy heart in the righteousness of Christ. The divine command is, *Believe on the Lord Jesus Christ;* the promise is, Whosoever believeth in him shall not perish, shall receive remission of sins, shall be justified from all things, shall have everlasting life. Why, then, dost thou lean to works, since salvation is by faith? Why dost thou disquiet thyself about attaining the righteousness of the law, and thereby suffer the law to disturb the peace of thy conscience, since thou hast a far better righteousness which ought to reign there, even the righteousness which is of God by faith? For thou art a believer, and although a weak one, yet thou hast as good a title to Christ and his righteousness as the strongest believer in the world; because thy right comes from the free grant of the word of grace, and is apprehended by faith, by which all things are become thine. Thou art an heir of them all, by faith in Christ Jesus. O thou of little faith! why then dost thou doubt? Remember how highly thou dishonourest the infinite love and free salvation of Jesus, and how much thou robbest thy own soul of its peace, and of its growth in grace, by thy weak and little faith. Think upon these things, and entreat the Author and Finisher of the faith to strengthen it in thy soul. But perhaps thou wilt say, How shall I so live upon Christ with my weak faith, that it may grow stronger, and I may get the better of my legal spirit? Here is the remedy— may it be to thee effectual! The Scripture directs thee to look at Christ God-man as thy surety, who for thee has wrought out a finished salvation; and whatever he has promised in his word relating to this salvation, thou art to trust him for the making of it good, and to depend upon his faithfulness and power to make it good to thee. Whatever, therefore, he has done and suffered to save thee from the curse of the law and from the spirit of bondage, and to make thee free with the liberty of the children of God, thou art to live upon him for these blessings, and by faith to be always receiving them from him in the fullest and largest measure that he promises them to thee. Look not into thyself, then, for any qualification, but look unto Jesus, that thou mayest experience more of that liberty wherewith he hath made thee free, and mayest be no longer a babe, unskilful in the word of righteousness. Hear what he says:—If the Son shall make you free, ye shall be free indeed: free from the law of sin and death, free from condemnation at the bar of God; and being freed from the bondage of corruption, ye shall be brought into the glorious liberty of the children of God; heirs of God, and joint heirs with Christ. This is the freedom which God promises thee; it is very extensive, has many noble privileges, and vast blessings. By faith all is thine. See how perfectly believers have received all; and may thy faith be like theirs! Rom. viii. 15, &c.: "Ye have not received the spirit of bondage again to fear; but ye have received the spirit of adoption, whereby we cry, Abba, Father. The Spirit itself beareth witness with our spirit, that we are the children of God; and if children, then heirs; heirs of God, and joint-heirs with Christ." Observe what is here said of the believing Romans, and by faith thou shalt experience the same as perfectly as they did.

1. They were freed from the spirit of bondage under which they once had laboured.

2. They were so freed as to be under it no more; they were not to fear again, as heretofore; for,

3. They had received the spirit of adoption, and he gave them the evidence of their sonship. Upon which,

4. They believed God was their reconciled Father, and they had boldness and access to him with confidence. And therefore,

5. They lived in light, and walked in love, like his children and heirs, who were to abide in his house for ever.

See also what great freedom the Galatians had, chap. iv. 4, &c. "God sent forth his Son made of a woman, made under the law, to redeem them that were under the law, that we might receive the adoption of sons. And because ye are sons, God hath sent forth the Spirit of his Son into your hearts, crying, Abba, Father; wherefore thou art no more a servant, but a son; and if a son, then an heir of God through Christ." O what treasures of grace and consolation are there in this scripture, tending to subdue thy legal spirit! Consider some of them.

1. All men having broken the law, and being under the curse of it, Christ was made under the law, that the law might reach him as the surety of his people; accordingly,

2. By his obedience to the precepts, and by his suffering the penalties of the law, he redeemed his people, who were under the law; so that,

3. They are no longer in bondage to it; but being made free, and having received the adoption of sons,

4. They have the spirit of liberty sent into their hearts to witness to them, that Christ fulfilled the law for them; and,

5. That the Father loves them, as his dear children, and they love him and serve him without fear, crying to him, Abba, Father:

6. Wherefore they are no longer servants in bondage to any one, but are made free indeed, being now the sons of God, through faith in Christ Jesus; and,

7. If sons, then heirs of God, and free to inherit whatever he has promised to give his children in earth and heaven.

These and many more arguments are contained in this one scripture, tending to subdue thy legal spirit, and to bring thee to live more comfortably by faith upon Christ, who, as thy surety, has fully kept the law for thee in his life and death. Thou art to consider thyself now, not under the law, but under grace, and therefore absolutely free from the condemning power of the law. This thou must maintain against all the carnal reasonings of thy legal spirit, *Christ is my law-fulfiller*. And thou wilt glorify him for redeeming thee from under the law, and wilt live in sweet peace in thine own conscience, while thou keepest fast hold of this most blessed and eternally precious truth. May all thy reading and prayer, and the use of all means, help thee to grow in the knowledge and experience of it!

There is a very strong bias and leaning in weak believers to a legal spirit, which ought to make them read such promises as I have been mentioning over and over again, that God may thereby encourage them to maintain the liberty which he hath given them in Christ Jesus, and to stand fast in it against the fresh attacks of the devil and unbelief. They should be always jealous over themselves, and watchful against their enemies; because, after they have in a truly gospel and evangelical way, through grace, got their legal spirit subdued; yet if it be not in the same way kept subdued, it will break out with more power than ever, and will be likely to bring them into bondage again to fear. And this may, and I have known it often happen, after they had obtained some great victories over it; and finding it not stir for some time, they flattered themselves they should have but little trouble with it any more. Thus they were drawn off their guard, which gave room to their legal spirit to exert itself again with vigour. This surprised the weak believers, put them upon reasoning and doubting whether all had been right with them before; and so at the very time when they should have taken the shield of faith, and should have been making use of it, they were questioning whether they had any; which left them unarmed in the midst of their enemies, an easy prey to every temptation; but an invisible power kept them safe, although they were not comfortable in themselves.

For the encouragement of persons in this case, that they may presently recover themselves out of the snare of the devil, they should observe, *First*, What the Scripture says of a legal spirit, describing it to be one of the members of their corrupt nature, one of the affections of the flesh, which will never be quite dead while the breath is in their bodies. It is an enemy that will be always fighting against the Holy Spirit; for they are directly contrary the one to the other; and therefore believers must not dream of any such victory as leaves no more fighting, but must expect sharp battles with their legal spirit, as long as ever they live. And, *secondly*, The same means by which they formerly obtained victory must be made use of again. As often as the legal spirit is tempting, Christ's strength must be opposed to it, and his strength must be brought into the soul by faith in his righteousness, as it is written, Isa. xlii. 24: "Surely shall one say, In the Lord have I righteousness and strength." Righteousness comes first, and is established in the conscience, that it may be pleaded and maintained there against all the charges and accusations of the law. And as often as these arise afresh, still they must be answered and silenced with this plea—In the Lord Christ have I righteousness; he is my law-fulfiller; and I depend upon his promised strength to make me stand fast in that liberty wherewith he hath made me free. And the soul must not only thus quiet and stay itself by faith upon the righteousness and strength of Christ for victory over the present temptation, but must also, *thirdly*, continually do this; because there is in our nature a continual opposition to it; the experience of which is the believer's safety. The abiding sense of his being naturally inclined to lean to legal dependencies, and therefore his want of Christ every moment, to justify him by his righteousness, and to keep him by his strength, will be the surest way to prevent his falling into bondage: for this will keep him very jealous over himself, and will show him the necessity of living out of himself for righteousness and strength; and while he liveth upon Christ for these by faith, he shall not be overcome by any enemy.

The glory of the incarnate God, and his infinite sufficiency to save, have not a greater enemy than a legal spirit; and therefore I have enlarged upon this point, that believers might be convinced from the word of God, they were saved from the condemnation of the law. They will never live comfortably till they see the law dead and buried, and then willingly give up themselves to be espoused to Christ, who will make them free indeed. And when they have learned of him to enjoy and walk in their Christian liberty, then they will be better acquainted with the warfare between nature and grace, the old man and the new, the flesh and the spirit, which warfare is the

Fourth great hinderance, that stops the growth of faith in weak believers. They are unskilful in it, soon tired of it, and often likely to be defeated. They do not enter into the battle strong in the Lord and in the power of his might, nor are they certain, if they fall in battle, they shall be saved with an eternal salvation. These are great discouragements; and until these be removed, they cannot fight the good fight of faith, like good soldiers of Christ Jesus. The case is thus: there is in every believer an old man and a new man—nature and grace, flesh and spirit; and these are opposite and contrary the one to the other in their principles and actions; they are always desiring different things, and pursuing different ends, which occasions a continual war between them. The flesh lusteth always against the spirit, and has many and mighty allies on its side, armies of lusts, the faculties of soul and body to bring forth sin, hosts of fallen angels, and all the world that lieth in wickedness. But the new man, renewed in the spirit of his mind, has a reconciled God on his side, and therefore he need not fear what any enemy can do unto him, but may bravely face the stoutest of them, even death itself, relying upon that sure word of promise, *I will never leave thee nor forsake thee.* Here is the believer's encouragement to fight, his God will never leave him. Here he obtains victory every day, his God never forsakes him; and after he has fought the good fight of faith, his God and Saviour will make him more than conqueror; he will send death to kill sin. And then the believer will never more have temptation from it, nor sorrow about it. But till that happy time come, he must be fighting against his corrupt nature and all its allies. No peace can be made with them, not even a truce. He must expect no kind of favour from them, because they are God's irreconcilable enemies; and therefore, as long as he is in the world, he must be fighting against the world; as long as he has a body of flesh, he must oppose it with its affections and lusts, because they war against the soul; and as long as he is in the reach of temptation, he must oppose the tempter, steadfast in the faith, never putting off his armour, until the Lord give him a discharge.

The believer's peace within, and victory without, are closely connected with the clear understanding of this case; and although I have stated it from the word of God and agreeably to the sense in which the church of God has always interpreted it, yet for its more full confirmation, some testimonies must be brought, which speak to the very point: first, to the believer's having in him an old man and a new; secondly, that these two are at war; and thirdly, that they fight together till death.

First,—The apostle says to the saints at Ephesus (iv. 22, &c.) : "Put off the old man, put on the new." Mind, the same persons had both in them an old man, corrupt according to his deceitful lusts, daily to be put off, and a new man to be put on, and renewed day by day in the spirit of his mind. The old man is described to have a body of sin with all his members, his affections and lusts; these must not be obeyed, but mortified. "Let not sin reign in your mortal body, that ye should obey it in the lusts thereof; neither yield ye your members as instruments of unrighteousness unto sin." (Rom. vi. 12, 13.) The saints at Rome had sin in them, and it wanted to reign as it had done heretofore in the lusts thereof; but,

Secondly,—They were not to obey them. There was in them a new man, who was to fight against those fleshly lusts which war against the soul. "The flesh lusteth against the spirit, and the spirit against the flesh: and these are contrary the one to the other, so that ye cannot do the things that ye would." (Gal. v. 17.) Here is battle between two, the flesh, the whole nature of the old man, and the spirit of the new man born again of the spirit: the cause of it is, the one wills what the other hates; each wants to carry his own will into execution; and these being contrary the one to the other, they fight for mastery; in the battle, the flesh, the old man, is defeated, and the spirit working in the new man conquers; and this lusting and fighting is in one and the same person, in him who is said to be not under the law, to be led by the spirit, and to live and to walk in the spirit. In Rom. viii. 7, the apostle calls the flesh the carnal mind; and he says, "It is enmity against God; for it is not subject to the law of God, neither indeed can be." Since it is enmity itself, there is no reconciling it; it will not, nay it cannot obey God, but is ever lusting and rebelling against his law. The nature of the battle is described at length in Rom. vii. The chapter consists of three parts,—first, the believer's liberty from the law, to ver. 6; secondly, he answers some objections made against the law from its nature and properties; and that in his own person, because it had been the means of bringing him to the right knowledge of sin (ver. 7); and sin being discovered by the law, through the corruption of nature, raged and rebelled the more in him (ver. 8); and the law had made him sensible of God's anger against sin, and of his deserving death and hell for it (ver. 9 to 14); and from thence to the end of the chapter, he describes the conflict between the old man and the new, the one consenting to the law, and the other resisting the law. In this conflict there were three sharp attacks; in the first he found in himself two contrary principles of action always resisting each other, the old man fighting against the new (from ver. 14 to 18); secondly, when the will of the new man was good, through the opposition of the old man, it had not the desired effect (ver. 19, 20); and thirdly, he felt in himself two contrary laws, both requiring obedience, the law of the members warring and rebelling against the law of God written in the renewed mind; for no sooner did his mind, guided by the Holy Spirit, set about anything which God's law commanded, but he found the law of the members making a strong resistance. This he groaned under, as a heavy burden, and was humbled for it before God, expecting pardon from him, and victory every day, and perfect deliverance at last.

I cannot enlarge upon this chapter. Turn to it, and read it over upon the plan which I have here laid down, remembering all along that St. Paul is describing himself; he ten times says it is himself he is speaking of, from ver. 7 to ver. 14, where he is showing of what use the law had been to him, when he was first convinced of sin; and from thence to the end, he mentions himself thirty-eight times. *I*, the apostle Paul, *I myself*, my very self, and not another; *I myself am*, now, at this present, at the very time of writing this; *I myself*, whom the law of the spirit of life in Christ Jesus hath made free from the law of sin and death; *I myself*, to whom now there is no condemnation, for I am *in* Christ Jesus, and I walk after the Spirit, am still at war with sin that dwelleth in me, with the old man, with the flesh, with the law of the members, with the body of sin. Although I have a new nature, and God is on my side, yet it is a hard and a sharp battle. I find it so. The length of it makes it still more painful, and forces me to cry out, " O wretched man that I am, who shall deliver me from the body of this death?" Paul was not out of God's favour, or accursed; but as the word rendered *wretched* means, he was weary and tired with this continual fighting, troubled with the filthy motions of sin rising and striving and rebelling in him, and giving him no rest: this was such a hard warfare that he was ever looking out and praying, " Who shall deliver me?" He meant wholly, perfectly, deliver me from this corruption. He sighed for it, not because he doubted of an absolute deliverance, but because he had sure and certain hope of it; not because he was ignorant who his deliverer was, but because he had steadfast faith in him. " Thanks be to God through Jesus Christ." This comforted him, and kept him fighting on with courage. He knew that he should gain the victory; and through Christ, not through his own virtues or works, but through faith in the life and death, in the blood and righteousness of Christ, he should at last be more than conqueror.

Since this was the case with the apostle, who can expect a discharge from this warfare until death? What! says one, is it to continue so long? Yes, the Scripture is very clear to this point, as I was thirdly to show.

The seat of the corruption of the old man, or of the flesh, is not only in our nature, but is also our very nature itself. That which is born of the flesh is flesh, altogether carnal and corrupt. It is a filthy fountain, always sending forth impure streams, and therefore, while the believer is in the body, he must either be fighting against the flesh, or else be led captive by it. We that are, says St. Paul, in this tabernacle of flesh, do groan, being burdened with sin and sorrow. And when did they expect an end of their groaning, and rest from their burdens? Not till the tabernacle was dissolved by death. Ourselves, says he, who have the first fruits of the Spirit, even we ourselves groan within ourselves, waiting for the adoption, to wit, the redemption of our body. The body will be redeemed from the grave, and raised like the glorious body of Jesus Christ; this is promised, and this we wait for; and until death deliver us from this mortal corruptible body, we shall be groaning under the burden of it. This was St. Paul's case. He had long sighed to be discharged from his warfare, and, like an old, weary, tired soldier, he wished the hard, tedious campaign was ended, that he might enter into rest; but hear with what joy he at last cries out, "I have fought the good fight." Have fought it? What! is the battle over? Yes, just over. "I am now ready to be offered, and the time of my departure is at hand—I have finished my course." My battle and my life are finished together; and so must thine, reader. Thou art to resist unto blood, striving against sin; for thou art called to fight the good fight of faith, until thou lay hold of eternal life. Since thou art a believer, however weak, and hast a new man in thee, as well as an old, they will be fighting against each other, till thou finish thy course. And if this discourage thee, consider what God has spoken concerning this warfare, and what exceeding great and precious promises he has made to them who are engaged in it. He has promised to pardon those corruptions of the old man, to subdue them, and to deliver thee from the very being of them. Canst thou desire more? Mark well what he says to thee, and be not faithless, but believing.

First,—Although the believer has an old man, corrupt according to the deceitful lusts, always warring against the new man, yet the Lord God has promised a free and a full pardon, because he has imputed sin, all thy sin, to the Son of his love, who bore it in his own body upon the tree. After the apostle, in Rom. vii., had described the battle between them, he makes this inference, "There is, therefore, now no condemnation to them who are in Christ Jesus," to them who are *in* Christ, united by faith as members to him their head, and thereby partakers of his righteousness, there is *now*, while they are fighting against their corruptions, no condemnation; "For," says he, "the law of the spirit of life in Christ Jesus hath made me free from the law of sin and of death." (Rom. viii. 2.) These words demonstrate that Paul was speaking of himself in the 7th chapter. Although he had the corruption of nature still in him, and was fighting against it, yet being in Christ by faith, he was made free from the guilt and punishment due to it; therefore he had, and every believer shall have, a full pardon. In consequence of which,

Secondly,—He shall subdue the corruptions of the old man. This is promised, and shall be made good. The Lord encourages believers to oppose the reign of sin in their mortal body, and not to obey it in the lusts thereof, with this promise, "Sin shall not have dominion over you." (Rom. vi. 14.) Ye are under grace, and grace is almighty to subdue sin, because it is atoned for. In like manner he says to the Galatians (v. 16), "Walk in the Spirit, and ye shall not fulfil the lusts of the flesh." Ye shall not fulfil them either in word or deed. The lusts of the flesh will be in you, but not one of them shall reign over you; the Spirit of Jesus will teach you to resist, and enable you to overcome them, yea, to crucify and mortify them day by day. And besides this, the Lord has promised,

Thirdly,—Deliverance from the very being of thy corruptions. The time is coming when they shall not exist in the believer, nor any more be suffered to tempt him. He shall be made holy and blameless, without spot or wrinkle of sin, or any such thing. In this perfect state the Father now sees him, and accepts him in the beloved, and after death admits the soul into his presence, cleansed with the blood, clothed with the righteousness, adorned with the graces of his dear Son; and body, soul and spirit shall be in this perfect state in the day of our Lord Jesus Christ—they shall be unblamable in holiness before God, even our Father, at the coming of our Lord Jesus Christ, with all his saints. It doth not yet appear how great a perfection of holiness this will be; but we know that when he shall appear, we shall then be like him, for we shall see him as he is. Such are the divine promises. And dost thou not see from hence, reader, what great things thou art to expect in thy present warfare? If thou sayest, How shall I attain all that is promised? Know that it is to come to thee by faith. Christ, and all that he has, is thine upon believing, and particularly a free pardon for indwelling sin, as well as for any other. Consider him as thy surety God-man, taking thy sins and sufferings upon himself to save thee from them. By his life and death he has obtained full salvation, which he gives to thee freely. And thou hast received it. Thou canst not deny but thou art a believer, and it is written, "All that believe are justified from all things;" from the corruption of their nature, as well as the corruptions of their lives. Know, then, that there is no condemnation to thee. The judge himself says so. And when he acquits, who shall lay anything to thy charge? Here thou must hold, through the power of the Lord, if thou wouldst have thy spiritual warfare successfully conducted. Abide by the sentence of God, and keep condemnation out of thy conscience. Have it ready to plead against all charges, from whatever quarter they come, that Christ hath made ME free from the law of sin and of death. Here I must refer thee back to what has been said concerning Christ and his finished salvation. Thou now seest how necessary it is thou shouldst be well established in the belief of his Godhead, and the infinite sufficiency of his salvation, so that he is both able and willing to save thee from all thy sins, and all the misery due to them, and to bestow upon thee eternal happiness, and to bring thee, by his almighty power, safe to the eternal enjoyment of it. All this he will give thee, not for working, but in believing. I entreat thee, therefore, to read again and again what has been before said upon these subjects; and the good Lord help thee to apply it to thy present case, that thou mayest be fully assured thou art in Christ, and that there is no condemnation to thee!

But perhaps thou art ready to say—Steadfastly do I believe all this; but I do not find such victory over my corruptions as I could wish; nay, I think at times they rage more than ever. Here thou forgettest the Lord thy strength. Thou dost not make use of him, and therefore thou failest. The woman with the bloody issue grew worse and worse till she went to Christ: so wilt thou. Why is it given thee to know Christ in the Spirit, but that thou shouldst go to him daily and plead his promise—Lord, thou hast declared that sin shall not have dominion over thy people: I believe this word of thine cannot be broken, and therefore, helpless in myself, I rely upon thy faithfulness to save me from the dominion of such and such a sin (as then tempts thee). Put forth thy power, O Lord Christ, and get thyself glory in subduing my flesh with its affections and lusts! And then trust him to make his word good, and wait the event. Sooner shall heaven and earth pass away, than sin, any sin thus left with Christ to be subdued, shall reign over thee.

If thou sayest, I think I seek for victory over sin in no other way, and yet I do not attain it so completely as I desire; depend upon it, thou art under some mistake; for Christ is almighty to fulfil every promise in its largest sense and fullest meaning, and there never was a believer who could justly charge him with the breach of his word. Perhaps thou dost believe, that power to subdue sin comes from Christ, and thou art expecting it from him; but hast thou not some legal dependence, some notion of thy own working together with him? Search and see. Dost thou commit ALL to the Lord, who is to do ALL and in ALL? Is the whole battle left to him,—wisdom, and courage, and armour, and strength, and patience, and victory, are all from the Lord? If thou art not doing this simply, thou art not living by faith upon Christ, but thou art fighting in thine own strength, and depending upon some inherent stock of grace, or knowledge, or experience. While these proud selfish motives put thee upon asking his help, he will not give it thee; because thou dost not wholly depend upon him for it.

Or perhaps Christ does not appear on thy side, because thou art proposing some wrong end. Thou art working and striving against sin to establish a righteousness of thine own, which is to be some part of thine acceptance before God; and thou hast been trying in thine own strength to get thy corruptions quite subdued; but they were too strong for thee, and therefore now thou art glad to make use of Christ's help. And if he would do the work for thee, then thou wouldst have confidence in the flesh, and this thy fancied holiness would be the ground of thy rejoicing before God. Is it not so? If it be, thou wilt never succeed upon this plan. Christ will not give his glory to another, nor put the crown of his gospel grace upon the head of thy legal dependence.

Or perhaps thou art expecting from Christ what he has not promised, such a victory over thy corruptions that they shall not fight again for some time, or that they shall be quite dead and buried. And so they shall be in the Lord's appointed time. But now he calls upon thee to fight against them; he provides thee armour for that purpose, even the whole armour of God; and he requires thee to resist unto blood, striving against sin, promising thee daily victory. This is thy present state of warfare. To this thou art now called, and there is no discharge in this war. O beware then, as thou lovest thy soul, of a false peace! Thou wilt be sadly deluded, if thou ever supposest that thy fighting is over, before thy course be finished. The good fight of faith must continue till death; for till then, corruption being in thee, thou must oppose it, relying upon God for promised victory over it. He is able to save thee from the very being of it now, as well as in heaven. But it is not his mind and will. Here

THE LIFE OF FAITH 57

he will have thee to live by faith, which is every moment to keep thee dependent upon Christ, or thou wilt fall. This is to exalt his grace, and to subdue thy selfish legal spirit; to humble thy pride, to put thee upon prayer and watchfulness, to make sin more hateful, and heaven more desirable; and to secure the glory of every victory to him, whose strength is perfected in thy weakness. These are some of his gracious purposes in keeping thee continually dependent upon his strength; and if he has made thee willing to fight and conquer, to the praise of the glory of his grace, then thou wilt experience that blessed promise—" sin shall not have dominion over thee." And it will not be long before sin shall not have a being in thee. Reader, if thou hast fallen into these or any other mistakes concerning the subduing of thy corruptions, mind what is written and what is promised. Having first received, through faith, in the blood of Christ, the pardon of thy sin, then, as one of his good soldiers, thou art to fight against it all thy life. He being on thy side, promises to subdue sin for thee.

Without him thou canst do nothing in this warfare, and therefore thy faith resting on his promise, is to wait the fulfilling of it. He has given thee his word that he will use his almighty power for this purpose. To that word must thou look, believing that Christ will bring thee victory continually, if thy faith fail not; greater, as thy faith increases; complete, when the good fight of faith shall be ended, and thou shall rest from thy labours. All this he stands engaged to do, and his power is able to fulfil his engagements, and thy faith will bring thee happy experience of his power. When corruptions rise, temptations are strong, enemies numerous, dangers on every side, that is the time to glorify Christ, by making use of his promised strength. Then put thy trust in the captain of thy salvation, and fear not. Look unto Jesus, and look at nothing but him. The battle is his. He will fight for thee, and thou shalt hold thy peace. Leave him to direct all, to do all, and to finish all relating to it, and then, as he can get all the glory, thou shalt see what a salvation he will bring thee. O that thy faith did but reach to the extent of his promises! How successful would be thy spiritual warfare, such victories over thine enemies, corruptions so subdued, the world so crucified, Satan so defeated, as thou canst now scarce believe. The Lord increase thy faith! Look up to him for it: because, as thy faith increases, let the battle grow hotter and hotter, thou wilt find thyself safer, and have more reason to give thanks to God, through Jesus Christ thy Lord.

For want of attending to the important truths already considered, and of bringing them into constant use and exercise, young believers are liable to fall into another great mistake, which keeps their faith weak, and stops its growth; namely, a hearkening to sense, and trusting to its reports; which is the fifth general head I purpose to consider.

They are seeking to be established, and they think that they should have no doubt of their being true believers, if they had but the testimony of sense, and comfortable feelings, to assure them of it. And being used to judge in this way in other matters, for it is our strongest evidence in natural things, they are disposed to expect the same in spiritual; and they are the rather disposed to it, because sensible comforts are promised in Scripture: which being very desirable and pleasing to nature, they are apt to covet them too much; and from not regarding what the Scripture says about them, they are apt to seek them in a wrong way, and for a wrong end. Sense judges from what it sees, and draws its inferences from what it feels: so that its report to the conscience, either of a believer's state, or of his growth in it, is not from unchangeable things, which would settle the conscience in peace, but from changeable things, which leave room for continual doubting. Sense also looks at the fruits of faith more than at the object of it: and if the believer has been misled and taught to confound these two together, he will be at great uncertainty in judging of his state; for instead of making the word of God, he will make his comforts the ground of his faith; and as these are more or less, so will his faith be, When he has comfortable feelings, then he will think himself a believer; and when he has none, then he will think himself an unbeliever; changing his judgment of himself as his feelings do, like the wind, and varying as his comforts do, like the weather. This is a commom case. I have seen the sad effects of it in the lives of many of my acquaintance, who, from being taught thus to judge of themselves, were tossed about for several years, up and down, now comforted, then doubting, and could not get any solid establishment, till the word and Spirit of God convinced them that sense was not to be the ground of their believing, nor the object to which they were to look. Sense judges by feeling, and reports what it sees. Sense says, Now I am in the favour of God: for I feel it. Now he is my God: for I find him so; I am comforted. Now he demonstrates it to me: for I feel nearness to him in prayer, and sweet answers. Now I am sure my duties and services are acceptable: for I am quite lively in them, and I come from them with warm affections. Now I cannot doubt; for I feel the assurance of his love to me. And when sense has lost those comfortable feelings, then it draws contrary inferences.—Now I am not in the favour of God: for I do not feel it. Now he is not my God: for I do not find him so; I am not comforted, &c.

What can be the issue of this, but continual wavering and changing? for our feelings are sometimes more, sometimes less, as every believer experiences. What an unsettled state then must he be in, who has no way to judge of himself, but by those changeable things? What room does he leave for continual doubting, and what trouble and misery does he thereby bring upon himself, as well as dishonour to the unchangeableness of God, in his nature and promises! If the poor, weak believer should say, I am convinced of this, and I should be glad to have my faith so fixed, that I might be freed from doubts and fears; then let it rest upon the word of God, which is the only ground of believing, and is therefore called the word of faith, upon which faith is built, and by which it is nourished and grows up. The believer should receive and rely upon what God hath spoken, and because he hath spoken it; for his word changeth not: it abideth the same for ever: therefore, what it truly reports, stands upon an immovable rock. Sense and feeling may report things contrary to it; but the believer can silence them with, *God has spoken it :* for his faith has evidence of things not seen; and he does not form his judgment by the things which are seen, but by the things which are not seen. Generally speaking, faith judges the very contrary to what sense does, and will not believe what sense perceives. Abraham, against hope, believed in hope; so do all his children. They believe the pardon of sin, victory over sin, and the death of sin; the immortality of the body, though crumbled to dust and atoms; the second coming of Christ, and the eternal state of happiness or misery. Faith looks at God's word, calling the things which be not, as though they were, and is commonly forced to contradict sense. Sense judges from what it sees,—faith from what God says; sense is governed by what appears,—faith by what God says shall be; sense looks inward,—faith looks outward: faith can answer the seeming contradictions which sense opposes to it, from the word of God, which cannot be broken; and, when sense is ready to despair, and all its fine frames and feelings are gone, then it is the believer's happy privilege still to trust in the Lord, and to have a good hope, because of the word of his grace.

But perhaps thou art ready to say, It is written, that there is great joy and peace in believing; yea, joy unspeakable and full of glory. True; these are what faith produces, and not what it is. These are the fruits of faith, which it brings forth in most abundance, from the inexhaustible fulness of Jesus. The more simple the believer is, the more he eyes Christ the object of faith, and the word the ground of faith, the more clear and distinct will the actings of his faith be, and consequently it will bring greater peace into the conscience, and more joy into the affections. But still these fruits are not faith; no more than the fruit is the tree. The fruits do not go before faith, but follow it, and grow from it. This is God's order. He gives us his word to be the ground of our believing; and by believing all things promised in the word are made ours, then we go on comfortably and are happy; but when sense is put in the place of the word, then the consequence is, that weak believers have got a changeable rule to judge of themselves by, which hinders them from being established in believing, and from attaining the promised peace and joy.

Some may begin to object, What! are you against all lively frames, and sensible comforts? No, God forbid. I would have them spring from the right cause, that they might be more pure and fixed than they commonly are. God's word and promises are an unchangeable foundation to rest upon, even when sensible feelings are gone, because Christ, revealed in the word, and laid hold of in the promises, changeth not. Therefore, reader, for thine own sake, and for the glory of God, take heed what thou buildest thy faith upon. Beware of making anything that sense reports to thee the ground of it, but rest it upon that which abideth for ever. The word of God is a sure foundation: it will never fail thee. Thou mayest safely depend upon it, because it cannot be broken, and steadfastly rely upon Christ to make its promises good to thee. There is thy object. Look at him. And since he is thine, thy Saviour and thy God, make use of him as such, and trust body and soul, and all things belonging to them, in his hands, and, among the rest, thy comforts. Be content he should give them to thee as seemeth him good. Set not thy heart upon them, nor follow him, as the multitude did, for the sake of his loaves and fishes, and the dainties that he gave them, who, when these were withheld, soon forsook their kind benefactor. Thou art by faith to make up all thy happiness in him, and in him only; and he himself being thine, let him give thee or take away what he will besides, thou hast enough. What! is not this comfort enough, that thou hast got the pearl of great price, the infinitely rich, inestimably precious Jesus? who has the wisdom of God to contrive what is best for thee, boundless love to dispose him, and almighty power to enable him to give it thee; and he has promised it; canst thou desire more? Walk then with him by faith, and not by sight. When the word of God is the ground of thy faith, which rests there, and is grown to a fixed settlement, then thou wilt be enabled to go on comfortably, whatever thy frames and feelings be; yea, when these are at the lowest ebb, thou wilt not be thereby discouraged. Suppose thou art walking in darkness, thou canst walk by faith, because thou hast a promise: "Who is among you that walketh in darkness, and hath no light? Let him trust in the name of the Lord, and stay upon his God." (Isa. l. 10.) Still let him trust and believe. Why? Because God is *his* God still. Mind that, his God still; this blessed relation still subsists, and faith may draw comfort from it in the darkest hour. Suppose thou art in heaviness through manifold temptations; the word says to thee, "Heaviness may endure for a night, but joy cometh in the morning." Here thou mayest quiet thy heavy heart, and rest with confidence, till the Lord deliver thee out of thy temptations. Suppose God hideth his face from thee, thou hast the example of those in the same case: "I will wait for the Lord that hideth his face from the house of Jacob, and will look for him." (Isa. viii. 17.) Wait in faith, looking for him, and thou shalt see the light of his countenance. Suppose all other comforts fail; thou hast one still, worth more than all—"This God is *my* God for ever and ever. He will never leave me nor forsake me." This is the happiness of the true believer; he is enabled to maintain his confidence, when sensible feelings are no more. And thou seest, reader, how this happiness is attained, and how it is preserved. It is by trusting to things which change not, the word of God, the Son of God, and his promises, all which are in him, yea, made in him, and in him, Amen, fulfilled by him. May the Lord help thee simply to trust his word, and to live upon Christ for the fulfilling of it; and then thou wilt indeed get, what thou art now seeking in vain, a comfortable frame, and wilt be enabled to maintain it against all the discouragements of sense. To that end, search the Scriptures, which are able to make thee wise unto salvation; and let it be thy daily request to the Lord to make thee strong in faith, that thou mayest not stagger at his promises through unbelief, but mayest against hope believe in hope. Beg of him, when sense goes contrary to the word, to enable thee still to believe it, and not to doubt of Christ's faithfulness to fulfil it—and ask for strength to walk every moment by faith, and not by sight. Thus the Lord will carry thee on safely and sweetly from faith to faith, till thou receive the end of thy faith, even the salvation of thy soul. May it be so. Amen.

St. Paul has been my guide hitherto. He says (Heb. v. 13), that a babe in Christ is one who is unskilful in the word of righteousness. To this determination of his, I have had an eye all along, and have accordingly endeavoured to remove those hinderances out of the way of young beginners, which chiefly arise from their unskilfulness in the word of righteousness. Righteousness signifies strict justice, with respect to God; it is paying him the full demands of his holy law: in this sense there is none of us righteous, no not one. The God-man Christ Jesus, the surety of his people, came to work out such a righteousness for them, and the word reveals it, sets it before them in its infinite freeness, and in its infinite sufficiency to justify from all things. The word is also the means in the hand of the Spirit, of bringing them with the heart to believe unto righteousness, and therefore the Scripture is called the word of righteousness; and being unskilful in it, signifies want of experience in the management of it, unskilful in the knowledge of the person of the Lord our righteousness; who is true and very God, as well as true and very man; unskilful in the nature of his righteousness, that it is absolutely perfect and everlastingly meritorious, so that any sinner, by receiving it, will be not only delivered from sin, and all the miseries due to sin, but will also be entitled to life and glory; unskilful in the gift of righteousness, how freely God bestows it, nothing being required to make it the sinner's, but receiving it, and therefore it is called the righteousness of faith: because by faith he crusts in it for salvation, and for all its blessings in earth and heaven, and expects them as the fruits of righteousness—unskilful in experience, not knowing how to plead this righteousness against the charges of the law, of conscience, and of the accuser of the brethren, and therefore apt to fall into a legal spirit, to be distressed in their warfare between the old man and the new, and to covet and to rely more upon sensible feelings, than upon the sure testimony of God in his word. These are some of the principal difficulties which young believers meet with, and they all arise from their unskilfulness in the word of righteousness; and therefore I have particularly considered some scripture motives for removing them out of the way. And after thou hast perused these motives, have they been the means of settling thy judgment, comforting thy conscience, and strengthening thy faith? Dost thou see more of Christ's grace and power to save thee a sinner, than thou didst before, and therefore canst trust him better, and in time of need make more use of his promised grace? If this be thy case, give him the glory, and may he carry thee on from strength to strength! But if thou hast received no improvement from reading thus far—what is the reason? Perhaps thou art under some of the temptations here described. Search, and see. And whatever it be, either in doctrine or experience, which hinders the increase of thy faith, may the Lord discover it to thee, and enable thee to overcome it, that thou mayest be no longer a babe unskilful in the word of righteousness, but mayest grow up to be a young man, strong in the Lord, and in the power of his might!

The apostle Paul has directed me how to speak to the babes in Christ; and another apostle shows how they grow up to be young men, and thereby he furnishes me with matter for the second part of this treatise on the Life of Faith: "I have written unto you, young men," says he, "because ye are strong, and the word of God abideth in you, and ye have overcome the wicked one." (1 John ii. 14.) These young men knew the principles of the doctrine of Christ; they were established in the belief of his Godhead, of the infinite sufficiency of his salvation, of the free gift of all its graces and blessings, promised to him that worketh not, and received by faith only, and all treasured up for the believer's use, in the fulness of Christ Jesus, to whom he is to bring nothing to recommend him, but the promise of the grace which he then wants, and a dependence upon Christ to supply that want. These young men had attained to a good degree of knowledge and experience in these truths. They began to be able to keep the evidence of their union with Christ clear and distinct, and to improve it by their communion with him in all his offices. But notwithstanding their establishment in these points, they had many temptations and great difficulties—still they knew but in part—still they had a fleshly corrupt nature to watch over and to fight against, always inclining them to trust to the law, to their feeling, to anything but Christ, and always disposing them to yield to the suggestions of the devil, and to the allurements of the world. This warfare, instead of ceasing, grows hotter and hotter, but they grow stronger. It is the peculiar character of the young men in Christ *to be strong:* they have learnt where their strength lies, and they put it forth. They go down to battle not trusting in any power or might of their own, but strong in the Lord, and in the power of his might. He is their strength. When the enemy cometh in like a flood, then to Jesus they look for safety and victory— " O our God, we have no might against this great company that cometh against us, neither know we what to do, but our eyes are upon thee." The abiding sense of their own weakness keeps them dependent upon him, so that the more they feel of their helplessness, the stronger they grow: because they live more upon Christ for strength, which illustrates that seeming paradox of the apostle, " When I am weak, then am I strong "—when I am most sensible of my own weakness, then am I strongest in the Lord; his strength is then perfected in me. And his strength is put forth in the effectual working of it by believing. It is not, neither can it be, inherent in them, who without Christ can do nothing, but it is brought in by faith ; nor does faith bring it in to lodge it, or lay it up in store, till it shall be wanted ; but when it is wanted, faith then regards the promise, looks up to Christ to fulfil it, and receives strength out of his fulness. And being his, freely promised, and freely given, it is therefore called the strength of grace. "Thou, therefore, my son," says Paul to Timothy, "be strong in the grace that is in Christ Jesus." Strong faith gets strong grace from Christ, according as it is written—"All things are possible to him that believeth;" for according to his faith it shall be done unto him. If his faith reach to the full extent of the promises, he shall find all things possible, which God hath promised, yea, he shall be able to do all things through Christ strengthening him.

This is the life of these young men in Christ. They are strong in him, living upon his promised strength, and by faith receiving it. They live not upon anything in themselves; but whatever they stand in need of, and whatever they have a promise for, that they expect shall be given them, by the power of God their Saviour. They see themselves poor helpless creatures, full of continual wants, and no means in their own power to supply them. The sense of this empties them of self-greatness and self-dependence, and the abiding sense of this keeps them humble and dependent upon Christ. Thus the Lord teaches them how to live out of themselves, and to be always receiving out of the Saviour's fulness grace for grace. They have his infinite storehouse to repair to, in which there is treasured up for them everything that they can possibly want. Happy for them, their God has promised to supply all their need out of the riches of his grace in Christ Jesus, and by faith they have an abundant supply to the praise of that God, who keepeth his promise for ever. In him they live—he is the Lord and giver of spiritual life, as Paul says—"I live, yet not I, but Christ liveth in me." They are made strong in him. "The Lord is the strength of my life," says the Psalmist (Psalm xxvii. 1). That life which I live by the faith of the Son of God has all its strength from him,—and is continued by his power—"For none can keep alive his own soul." (Psalm xxii. 29.) "It is God who holdeth our soul in life." (Psalm lxvi. 9.)

And is kept by faith—"Ye are kept by the power of God through faith." (1 Pet. i. 5.) Whatever strength the believer wants, to enable him to bear hardship, endure the cross, fight his spiritual enemies, daily gain victories over them, he expects it from God, and through faith he receives it, and is kept—yea, so kept as to be confirmed unto the end. He that is able to keep believers from falling, will keep them until they receive the end of their faith, even the salvation of their souls. Thus the life which Christ begins by his grace, he continues by his strength; and every act of this spiritual life is from him. The will, the power is his; for he doeth all, and in all. These young men were so well assured of this, that they lived upon Christ for strength, and they received it; they were strong in him. Their faith viewed him in his exalted state with all power in heaven and earth, and engaged as their covenant head to use it for them, to make them and to keep them alive to God. On this power they depended; and whatever promise they had of its being used in their behalf, and pleaded it out at the throne of grace, and trusted Christ with the fulfilling of it, he never disappointed them. They were made strong, and stood fast in the Lord, who never withdrew his supporting arm; therefore they never ceased to put their whole trust and confidence in him.

When the enemy sees them thus strong in the Lord through faith, it stirs up his devilish malice, and makes him burn with envious rage. He leaves no temptation untried to draw them from Christ. He is well skilled in cunning wiles and sly devices for this purpose. He does not begin with tempting them to open sin; that would at once discover his wicked design; but he artfully tries to sap the foundation, and to weaken their faith. If he can get them from their dependence upon Christ, he carries his point; and too—too often he succeeds. Oh, beware, reader, of everything; suspect it, let its appearance be ever so fair and good, which in the least tends to weaken thy fast hold of Christ. Cleave to him with full purpose of heart, as long as ever thou livest: for the enemy's whole plan is to separate thee from him.

Formerly he tried to do this by distressing thee about thy sins—how they could be pardoned—whether being so great, so many, the blood of Christ could cleanse from all: now thou hast through believing received forgiveness of sins, he will try to do the same by distressing thee about thy duties. Sometimes he will try to bring guilt into thy conscience, by suggesting to thee thy many failings and shortcomings in them—the disorder of thine imagination—thy wanderings in thy prayers— thy dulness in hearing and reading the word—the little life and power thou findest in thine attendance upon the ordinances, and the coldness of thy love to God and man. If he can get thee to dwell upon these things, so as to forget Christ, then he has made way for this insinuation—How could it be thus with thee, and thou a strong believer? And if he can get thee to reason upon it, then he has thee fast, thou art catched in his snare. But if the Lord has taught thee not to be ignorant of Satan's devices, as soon as the thought arises, whether thou art in Christ, because of such failings, thou wilt know from what quarter it comes, and wilt immediately resist it. So, that the temptation will make thee stand faster: it will drive thee closer to Christ, make thy dependence stronger on his blood and righteousness; put thee upon making more use of him as thy intercessor and advocate with the Father, and help thee to live more out of thyself by faith upon him. Thus Christ becomes precious, thou art more humble: the snare is broken, and thou art delivered. When the enemy sees this, his implacable malice will soon tempt thee again. He has another deep-laid stratagem relating to thy duties, and that is from their being unsuccessful. Thou hast had something laid much upon thy heart, and thou hast carried it to God in prayer, and thou hast waited long, but no answer comes. Upon this, Satan takes occasion to suggest—Now you see God does not give you what you ask; although he has promised, Ask and ye shall have; the fault cannot be in him, therefore it is plain you are not in his favour; his promises do not belong to you. And if he can thus work a little upon thy impatience, he will soon get thee into doubting and unbelief. Here thou mayest see how all the wiles of Satan tend to one point; namely, to separate thee from Christ, and how necessary then is it that thou shouldst have this settled beyond all question that Christ and thou are one? If this be maintained in thy conscience, then Satan's stratagem is defeated: for Christ being thine, he will give thee everything that he has promised; and although thou hast it not just at the time thou hast fixed thyself, yet he knows best. Thou shalt certainly have it, if his infinite wisdom sees it good for thee; and if he does not see it good, his love will give thee something better. Thy faith must wait God's time. Strong faith can wait long. Having such a promise as this to depend upon — "They shall not be ashamed to wait for me" (Isa. xlix. 23), thou mayest with confidence wait, and be a follower of them, who through faith and patience inherit the promises; who by faith regarded the promises, by patience waited for the fulfilling of them; and although they waited long, yet they succeeded at last, and did inherit every grace and blessing for which with faith and patience they had been waiting. Go, and do thou likewise. Upon the failing of these temptations, the enemy has another ready. Since he cannot get thee off thy guard, by bringing thee into doubting and unbelief, he will attack thy faith in another way. He will come like an angel of light, and seem to be Christ's friend and thine. He will allow thee to be a child of God, and to be strong in faith. The more clearly thou art satisfied of thy union with Christ, the more will he improve, if thou art not aware, this thy certainty to his own wicked purposes. He will try to keep thine eye upon thy great graces and high gifts; he will flatter thee exceedingly upon them, and will tempt thee to view them with a secret delight, every now and then insinuating what a great Christian thou art—how few there are like thee—to what an exalted state thou hast attained—what temptations thou hast overcome—what victories thou hast gained over Satan—and how safe thou art now, fast upon the rock! And if he finds this pleasing bait is not instantly rejected with a—Get thee behind me, Satan, then he will begin to work upon thy self-love, and to give thee many plausible reasons for self-admiration, so that thou shalt first look pleasingly at, then fondly love, and at last sacrilegiously dote upon thy wondrous attainments. Thus he will lift thee up with pride, and will try to draw thee into his own crime, and into his own condemnation. What a dangerous temptation is this! How many have I known who fell into it! If thou sayest, By what means shall I escape it? Mind the first approach: for it is coming upon thee as soon as thou beginnest to think of thyself more highly than thou oughtest to think. Thou art in thyself a poor, miserable, helpless sinner, and to this very moment without Christ thou canst do nothing. Thou canst not do one good thing, nor overcome the weakest enemy, nor take one step in the way to heaven, without Christ: nay, thou canst not think one good thought without him. What hast thou then to be proud of, and to stir up thy self-admiration? Nothing but sin. The humble abiding sense of this tends to thy safety; for while this is ever present with thee—"In me, that is, in my flesh, dwelleth no good thing," it will lead thee to live by faith upon Christ for all good things. And being all his, and received every moment from him as his free gift, thou wilt be glorifying and exalting him in all, and for all; knowing that he resisteth the proud, but he giveth grace unto the humble. The Lord keep thee humble, and then thou wilt have grace to escape this cunning wile of the devil.

If thou shalt say, Alas! I am fallen into it; how shall I recover myself? Remember his case who in his prosperity said he never should be moved, the favour of the Lord had made his mountain to stand so strong. (Psalm xxx. 6, 7.) He was too confident in himself, and was moved. How did he recover his standing? "I cried unto the Lord, and unto the Lord I made my supplication. Hear, O Lord, and have mercy upon me, Lord be thou my helper." His prayer was heard; he found mercy to pardon his offence, and help to raise him up; and his mourning, he says, was turned into joy and gladness. Look up as he did to the Lord Christ. Plead thy pardon through his promised mercy, and beg of him to enable thee to walk more humbly with thy God. Then shall the Psalmist's experience be thine, and thou shalt escape the snare which was laid for thy precious life.

These young men having thus overcome the devices which Satan had contrived to weaken their faith, must expect a fresh attack from him. He will tempt them concerning the ground of faith. He sees they are strong, because the word of God abideth in them, therefore he will use all his cunning and power to weaken their trust in the word and promises of God. By the incorruptible seed of the word, faith is begotten; and by the same word it is nourished up and strengthened, growing exceedingly from faith to faith. The word, which is the sole ground of faith, reveals the covenant made by the eternal Trinity for the salvation of sinners, and makes many free promises of every covenant blessing to him that believeth. These promises may most steadfastly be relied upon, because of the unchangeable nature of God, who makes them. All his perfections are engaged for the fulfilling of his word; so that what he has spoken has an actual being and existence. He says, and it is done—saying and doing are the same with him. Let there be ever so great a distance of time between the word spoken and the thing done, yet this is as real as anything now in being; because it exists in the mind and will of God, is revealed in his word, and by his faithfulness and almighty power is to be established at the time appointed. How is it possible then that this word should be broken? There is no matter of fact of more undoubted evidence, nothing in futurity, not even the rising of the sun to-morrow, so fixed and certain as the accomplishment of God's promises to him that believeth. These young men in Christ were most assuredly persuaded of this truth. They knew that heaven and earth should pass away before one tittle of God's promises should fail. They looked upon them all as made in Christ, in him Yea, and in him Amen; made in him, and fulfilled to him, as the head of the body the church, and in him fulfilled to all his members. As certainly as every one of them has been made good to him the head, so will they be made good to his members. He has all power in heaven and earth committed to him for that very purpose. Whoever by believing is joined to him, he has thereby a right and title to every promise, and may boldly sue it out in time of need: and then it is Christ's office and glory to fulfil the promise. If mountains of difficulties stand in the way, the believer need not fear or doubt. Christ is upon the throne. What are difficulties against his almightly power? Besides, Christ has already given him good security. He has put into his hands the pledges and earnests of the promised inheritance, and how is it possible he should fail in fulfilling his engagements, and putting him in due time into actual possession? Read what the apostle says of this subject. Turn to the passage; for it is too long to quote, Heb. vi. from verse 11 to the end of the chapter; in which you may observe these particulars:—

1. The heirs of promise are apt to be full of doubt, and to have strife in their consciences about their right and title to all the graces and blessings of salvation.

2. God was willing, out of his infinite mercy, to establish their right and title to them beyond dispute, and to put an end to all strife.

3. Therefore he engaged, by promise, to give them all those graces and blessings, and,—

4. To show the unchangeableness of his will herein, he confirmed the promise by an oath.

5. It is impossible that God should lie in his promise, or that he should be perjured in his oath.

6. Therefore, here are two immutable things to strengthen the faith and hopes of the heirs of promise.

7. While their faith rests upon those immutable things, it will always bring them strong consolation.

8. When enemies, dangers, and temptations attack them, they are safe, by fleeing for refuge to lay hold of the hope set before them in God's immutable promises.

9. This hope will be as useful to them at such times as an anchor to a ship. By it they will ride out all the storms of life, until Jesus, their forerunner, bring them within the veil, where their anchor is now cast, and put them into eternal possession of all the promises.

With what rich and copious matter does this scripture abound, tending to show the absolute safety of resting upon God's promises! How strong are the arguments to persuade the heirs of promise to put their whole trust and confidence in the faithfulness of their God! who, having provided an infinitely glorious and everlasting inheritance for them, was willing to make it over to them in the strongest manner of conveyance, and therefore he has given them the promise and the oath of God, which cannot possibly change or alter, that their faith might never doubt or waver, and their hope might at all times be sure and steadfast. And, until he bring them to the inheritance itself, he has given them many sweet and blessed promises of all things needful for their temporal and spiritual estate, upon which he would have them not only to live comfortably at present, but also to receive them as part of the inheritance, allowed them for their maintenance till they come to age and enter upon the possession of the whole. And what God intended in his promise and oath, has its effects in a good degree among those who have the word of God abiding in them. They cast their anchor where he commands them, and they are not only safe, but also, in time of the greatest troubles and temptations, have strong consolation. When enemies come, corruptions arise, and difficulties are in the way, they have a promise and a promise-keeping God to depend upon. Whatever straits they are in, the word abiding in them brings some promise of support and deliverance: the promise shows what God has engaged to do, and faith receives the fulfilling of his engagements. When they draw nigh to God in duties—in ordinances, they know what he has promised to them that wait upon him, and they judge him faithful who hath promised; and lo! he is present with them.

In short, while they live like themselves, as the heirs

of promise, they are preserved from all evil, and want no manner of thing that is good. This is their happy case, thrice happy, because the means used to deprive them of their happiness are overruled of God for the establishing it. The enemy rages against them, but in vain: he was a liar from the beginning. The word is truth, and he abode not in it; therefore he hates it, and with a greater hatred, because the Lord has made it the means of strengthening those believers. He knows that all his temptations will be fruitless while the word abideth in them. He fears no weapon formed against him, like the sword of the Spirit; he has felt its sharpness and its power; with it the Captain of our salvation cut Rahab, and wounded the dragon; and with it all his good soldiers resist the devil, and make him flee from them. For these reasons he has great variety of temptations to weaken the believer's trust in the word and his reliance upon the promises of God.

Sometimes he attacks them in a matter where his hopes are founded in their ignorance: he is cunning to spy out the particular way in which they have been led, and their readiness to maintain their ground, by making use of the promises suited to that way. He resolves, therefore, upon some new temptation, with which they have never been exercised; and he watches the favourable opportunity to inject it with all his strength. Upon his doing it, the soul is put into a great hurry, because it has no promise ready to apply to the present case; for want of which, the understanding is confused, faith wavers, doubt enters, and Satan carries his point. This demonstrates the necessity of searching the Scriptures, and meditating upon them night and day. In them, God has graciously treasured up all sorts of promises. There is not a possible case for a believer to be in of spiritual or temporal concern, but there is a promise suitable to it, which he ought to have ready against the hour of temptation. If he has not, he neglects the Lord's kind provision, and lays himself open to the enemy's attack. Reader, if thou wouldst not be ignorant of Satan's devices, follow Christ's counsel—search the Scriptures. Remember, they are able to make thee wise unto salvation, through faith in Christ Jesus; therefore store up his promises; pray him to sanctify thy memory to retain them, and to enable thee to make use of them in every time of need.

If this temptation fail, the enemy will soon have another ready. I have known him often try, and often succeed, in endeavouring to take off the attention from the most easy parts of Scripture, and to fix it upon those parts which are hard to be understood. Upon those, the believer dwells too much, and puzzles himself. His head grows confused. He consults commentators, and they confuse him more. And if he does not fall from hence into questioning the truth of Scripture, yet he certainly neglects the right use of it, forgetting it is the means of building himself up in his most holy faith.

Reader, whenever thou art tempted about difficult texts, look up to the incarnate Word, and pray him by his Spirit to open thine understanding, that thou mayest know what thou readest; and if thou still dost not find the meaning of them made plain to thee, pass them by for that time. Do not puzzle and distress thyself about them. Perhaps when thou meetest with them again, they will appear easy, and Christ will give thee light to see and to comprehend them. If thou sayest, I do look up to him to teach me, but, nevertheless, I find many hard and difficult texts; remember thou knowest but in part, and therefore thou standest in need of daily teaching.

These texts are profitable, if they humble thee, and make thee live more upon the teaching of the divine prophet. The humbler thou art, thou wilt be the more teachable. The lower thou sittest at his feet to hear his words, thou wilt learn the most. The master himself has declared, "Whosoever shall humble himself as a little child, the same is the greatest in the kingdom of heaven." If these difficult texts thus humble thee, and make thee live more upon Christ's inward teaching, they will be the means of thy growth in saving knowledge. Thy hearing and reading the word in a constant dependence upon him, will keep thee from the dangerous errors and heresies of the times. Most of those arise from unlearned and unstable men, full of pride and self-conceit, whom God resisteth: but he giveth grace to the humble.

If he has given thee grace to hold fast the form of sound words, which thou hast learned and been assured of, the enemy will change his attack, and pursue thee with new temptations. Envious of thy happiness, he will be often assaulting thee, and trying to move thee from thy steadfastness. He will at times insinuate every lie that he can raise against the word of God, and he will not begin with reason or argument, but by way of surprise, with sudden injections, darting into the mind doubts like these—How do I know the Scripture is inspired? What proof have I? And if these be not immediately rejected, he will follow them like lightning with others:—How can that be inspired which is full of contradictions, and full of doctrines above reason? Who can defend the matters of fact related in it? The language is low and mean, unworthy of God—the Scripture is false—perhaps there is neither God nor devil.

These blasphemous thoughts sometimes put the believer into a hurry and confusion, and through the suddenness and violence of them greatly distress him. The apostle calls these assaults "the fiery darts of the wicked one"—darts, because he throws them with all his might against the soul; and fiery, because he would have them to catch hold of, and to inflame its corruptions and lusts. And they do, if the shield of faith be not ready to stop their force, and to quench their fire. This is a piece of the armour of God prepared for the believer's safety at such times, and the right use of it is this—The Lord having promised to be a shield to them that put their trust in him, and to compass them about with his favour, as with a shield, the believer looks up when these fiery darts are flying thick about him, and says—" O Lord God of hosts, who hast promised that thy faithfulness and truth should be my shield and buckler, now establish thy word unto thy servant. In thee, O my God, do I put my trust, save me in this hour of temptation."

Then the battle becomes the Lord's. He is engaged to put forth his strength to shield thee from the enemy.

Thus thou shalt conquer, and shalt happily experience what is written—" Resist the devil, and he will flee from you." He will flee for a season, but will return again. He has other temptations, and he will try them all to disparage the word of God, and to lessen the believer's confidence in it. Sometimes he will insinuate —How can these things be?—in what way or by what means can such a promise be fulfilled?—If you begin to reason upon the point, he will get you from your stronghold and conquer you. Beware of his lies, and have always your answer ready—" It is written." What God hath said, put your trust in, if all the world gainsay it: for he is faithful who hath promised, and all things are possible with him.

If this temptation does not succeed, and he cannot bring you to doubt of the truth of the promises, then he will try you about your right to them. When you are in darkness or walking heavily, in sickness or any trouble, and you have been praying for deliverance, but Christ does not presently answer you, then he has a favourable opportunity to suggest—Now you see the promises do not belong to you; Christ will not hear you; and therefore you have been deceiving yourself with a vain notion of faith. This is a common temptation, against which still oppose—" It is written." Thy case, be it what it will, has a promise, either of support or deliverance. If thou art not delivered, yet if Christ support thee, so that thy faith and patience fail not, does not this show his infinite goodness to thee? He will have thy faith tried, and he will put it into the fire, not to consume it, but that it may come like gold out of the furnace, purer and brighter. And what if thou art in the fire a great while? thou wilt see more of his tender mercies in keeping thee there, and wilt thereby learn to live in a more simple dependence upon him. Cast not away, therefore, thy confidence in the written word. The promises in it stand faster than the strong mountains. If all the powers in earth and hell should join, they cannot defeat one single tittle of them. When the world and all the works therein shall be burnt up, and the place of them shall be no more found, then the promises shall stand fast as the throne of God, and shall receive their full and perfect accomplishment through the ages of eternity.

These are some of Satan's temptations against the young men in Christ, who are strong, because the word of God abideth in them. His design is to weaken their reliance upon its promises. Till he can do this, he despairs of success, and therefore he tries every method which his wicked cunning and rage can invent. His busy active spirit is night and day plotting against the word of God. See a lively picture of his utter hatred to it in the parable of the Sower. While the good seed is sowing, the devil is indefatigable in picking it up. He exercises all his wiles to keep it out of the hearers' hearts, and he prevails with the greater part to reject it. Among those who seemingly receive it, he cheats three out of four, so that the word does not take root, nor bear fruit to perfection. Since Satan is thus successful, is it not absolutely necessary, reader, that thou shouldst be well acquainted with his devices? And the word abiding in thee, the ingrafted word, will both make thee acquainted with them, and also strong to resist them: because then thou wilt be taught by Christ's wisdom, and strengthened by his almighty power.

As thou growest in the sense of thy want of him, and livest in a closer dependence upon him, thou wilt understand more of his word, and experience more of his power. By which means, the enemy's continual attacks driving thee to Christ for the fulfilling of his promises, will make thee continually safe. Let the roaring lion rage, what hast thou to fear? Let him go about seeking whom he may devour, the Lord is thy shield and thy defence: in him is thy trust. Thou hast his promise that he will preserve thee from all evil, and will make all things, even Satan's spite and rage against thee, work together for thy good.

How dear and precious, then, should the word of God be to thee! If thou art weak, because it is the means of thy growing, and being nourished up; and if thou art strong, because by its abiding in thee thou wilt be established. May it be thy study and thy delight, and may every reading of it bring thee to a better acquaintance with, and a greater dependence upon, the adorable Jesus! And if thou desirest thus to profit from the Scriptures, I would advise thee, reader, to observe two things, which will be much for Christ's glory and for thy edification.

First,—In thy frequent and careful perusal of the Bible (and mind, thou canst not read it too much), take particular notice of the promises which are most suited to thy age, state, and condition in life: because these God has graciously made for thy use, and about these the enemy will be most busy with thee. Treasure them up then in thy memory, and have them ready against the time of need, looking up,

Secondly,—To Christ for the fulfilling of them. All the promises are made in him, and made good by him: thou art, therefore, in an humble dependence upon his faithfulness and power, to expect whatever thou wantest, and he has promised. Trust him, and he will not fail thee. Stagger not at any of his promises, through the seeming impossibility of their being made good, but depend upon his almighty power, and thou wilt find him a faithful promise-keeping God, whose word standeth fast for ever and ever. Thus thou shalt not only be safe, but shalt also overcome the wicked one, which the apostle John makes the last part of their character who are strong in the Lord. They overcome him by the strength of their faith. They hold fast their confidence in the Lord's promised strength, and he fights for them. That mighty arm, which bruised the serpent's head, brings them victory, as it is written of that noble army, mentioned Rev. xii. 11: "They overcame the accuser of the brethren by the blood of the Lamb, and by the word of their testimony."

Through faith in his blood they were pardoned and justified freely, and they knew that in him they had righteousness and strength, therefore they were at peace with God, and the accuser of the brethren could not lay anything to their charge. Thus they were delivered from his power, and translated into the kingdom of God's dear

Son; and they testified this by adhering to the word of truth. They believed that whatever Christ had therein promised he would fulfil to them and, they bore their testimony to their being safe in depending upon his word in the most trying circumstances. They would not give it up, whatever they lost for trusting to it; nay, they stuck steadfastly to its truth, although it cost them their lives for maintaining their testimony: for it is said of them, "they loved not their lives unto the death;" that is, they loved the truth more than life; they were not afraid publicly to own that their trust and confidence was in the blood of the Lamb; and they believed that they should be infinite and everlasting gainers by holding fast the word of their testimony unto death. And the Lord was with them, and mightily strengthened them, so that they joyfully sealed their testimony with their blood, although they died in flames, and in the most exquisite torments. Thus they overcame Satan.

A most noble company of those conquerors are now standing round the throne of the Lamb, enjoying his exceeding great and precious promises: he has crowned them with glory; he has clothed them with robes, washed and made white in his own blood; he has wiped away all tears from their eyes, and taken all cause of sorrow from their hearts; he has put palms into their hands, to show that they are eternal conquerors, and that they shall stand confirmed in bliss for ever and ever. May thou and I, reader, ere long, join them!—and until that happy time come, may our faith be daily more established in the blood and righteousness of the Lamb of God, that we may be growing in our love to him, and in our dependence upon him, until he admit us to see him as he is!

Through much exercise and fighting, these young men, strong and mighty in the Scriptures, grow up to be fathers in Christ; whose character is thus drawn by the apostle John (1 Epis. ii. 14): "I have written unto you, fathers, because ye have known him that is from the beginning," namely Jesus Christ, whose style and title it is to be from the beginning, as he himself speaks in Prov. viii. 22, 23: "The Lord possessed me in the beginning of his way, before his works of old. I was set up from everlasting, from the beginning, or ever the earth was." He was a person in the Godhead, co-equal and co-eternal with the Father, but was set up in his office-character from everlasting, to be the beginning of the ways and works of God. Upon account of what he was to do and suffer in man's nature, according to the grace of the covenant of the ever-blessed Trinity, he was the Creator and is the Preserver of the universe: for by him were all things created that are in heaven, and that are in earth, visible and invisible, and by him all things subsist: and he is the beginning, the first cause of all things in nature, and also in grace, the head of the body the church.

In the same manner our Lord speaks of himself, Rev. i. 8:—" I am Alpha and Omega, the beginning and the ending, saith the Lord, which is, and which was, and which is to come, the Almighty." He is in and from the beginning, being the first cause of all the divine works in creation, in providence, and in redemption, the Author and the Finisher, the First and the Last in all; which shows the great propriety of describing him here by this name. The apostle is treating of the highest state of a believer, and he says, it consists in knowing that Jesus Christ is all and in all. Whatever good there is in his kingdom of nature, from him it had its beginning, and by him it is preserved: whatever good there is in his kingdom of grace, he is the author of it; by his power it is continued; and when brought to perfection, he is the finisher. He is the beginning, he is the ending of all the counsels, and of all the works of God.

In this light these fathers had learned to consider the Lord Jesus: they knew that he was to do all for them, and in them, and by them: they not only knew it speculatively, but had also experimental knowledge of it. "Ye have known him that is from the beginning," have known him, and tried him, and found him to be what his name signifies. And this is the right knowledge of Christ—not such as the devil has; he could say, I know thee who thou art, the Holy One of God—not such as too many nominal Christians have, who profess that they know God, but in works they deny him—not such as many professors attain, for whom it had been better not to have known the way of righteousness, than after they had known it to turn from it. These fathers knew Christ by the inward teaching of his Word and Spirit, whereby he made himself known to them, as he does not to others. For he fulfilled to them the great promise of the new covenant—"I will give them a heart to know me, that I am the Lord; and they shall be my people, and I will be their God." (Jer. xxiv. 7.)

The covenant is well ordered in all things, and sure; particularly with respect to the quickening of the soul from a death in trespasses and sins, and to the renewing of its faculties, that they may be capable of knowing God; and to the enlightening them, that the light of the glorious gospel of Christ may shine unto them, even unto the heart, enlivening it with holy and heavenly affection to the person, to the offices, and to the glories of the blessed Immanuel. Whereby the believer, thus taught of God to know him aright, can now trust him, hope in him, and love him: which graces are strengthened from the consideration of God's standing related to him as his covenant God, and of his being one of God's redeemed people; from which relations he has a right to, and by faith may enjoy every covenant mercy in time, and shall be a partaker of them all in eternity.

This is the knowledge, concerning which so many and such great things are spoken in Scripture, and which St. John says these fathers had received: they had attained, by the Spirit of Wisdom and revelation to that knowledge of Christ, which is life eternal; and the same Spirit enabled them to be continually growing and increasing in the knowledge of Christ. As he shines more clearly into their hearts, he discovers to them more of their wants; he makes them better acquainted with themselves, and lets them feel more of the workings of their corrupt nature, and of their own entire helplessness.

Thus by his light they see deeper into that mystery of iniquity which is in them, and they grow in the sense and experience of it all their lives. Day by day, some failing, short-coming, infirmity or temptation leads them to more lowly and humbling views of themselves, and brings them fresh discoveries of their fallen and helpless state. While they attend to what is passing in their own breasts, every moment something will be speaking for Christ—"Without me ye can do nothing." It is this abiding sense of their wants, and faith in his promises to supply them, which lead them to be constantly looking unto Jesus. Many wants do not discourage them, for his promises are as many as their wants can be—nor great wants, for he has given them exceeding great promises—nor continual wants, for he has promised them grace every moment.

As they grow in the knowledge of themselves, they see more need of living upon Christ in the several offices which he sustains. The daily experience which they have of their own ignorance, and sinfulness, and helplessness, endear to them their divine prophet, priest, and king. The continual sense of their want of him makes them glad to live in a settled fixed dependence upon his fulness, and to be always receiving out of it. They would not live otherwise if they could. They know that their dear Saviour will manage better for them than they could for themselves. He has taken their affairs, spiritual and temporal, into his hands, and he can make no mistakes. His infinite love is guided by unerring wisdom, and its blessings are bestowed by almighty power. Happy for them, they and theirs are under the care of this best of friends. They knew it, and are sensible of their happiness.

Daily experience brings them fresh proofs of the love and power of Jesus; which makes them wish for more, still more faith, that they may glorify their blessed Saviour by trusting him more. However, in this they are growing, increasing day by day in their knowledge of the salvation, and gaining a closer acquaintance and fellowship with the person of God their Saviour, until they come to see him as he is.

This is the character of those believers who are steadfast in the faith, and are become fathers, able now to teach others also. They have attained to that knowledge of Christ, which is life eternal, and they are daily pressing forward. What they already know of him increases their desire to know more. And by being always conversant with him (for without him they can do nothing), they have continual opportunities of making new discoveries. In him are laid up treasures of everything that is great and good. His riches are unsearchable, infinite, and eternal. There is no coming to the end of them. Believers are persuaded of it, and therefore they try to dig deep into this golden mine. It is all theirs. The farther they go, the more is their faith strengthened, and the more precious Christ becomes; for they find such an excellency in the knowledge of Christ Jesus their Lord, that their souls hunger and thirst to know more of him. The more they attain, the more the appetite increases, and nothing can perfectly satisfy it, but the full enjoyment of Christ in glory, when they shall know, even as also they are known. Till that blessed time come, they will be growing in grace, and in the knowledge of God their Saviour.

This is the distinguishing mark of these fathers; they are pressing forward. They have not yet attained to the perfect knowledge of Christ, but they are going on to perection: and they make a happy progress. God meets them in, and blesses the means which he has appointed for their daily growth. In those, he requires them to depend and to wait upon him, and he gives them clearer discoveries of the adorable person, and of the gracious offices of the Lord Christ, and thereby enables them to live more by faith upon him for all things belonging to their temporal, their spiritual, and their eternal concerns. These particulars will include the principal acts of the Life of Faith, and while we take a short view of them, may every page, reader, be made the means of increasing and strengthening thy faith in the Lord Jesus!

First, they grow in the knowledge of his person, which is altogether wonderful; so that they can never come to the end of his perfections, nor to eternity can they show forth all his praise; for he is God and man in one Christ—Jehovah incarnate—Immanuel, God with us. This is the great mystery of godliness, God manifest in the flesh; in which he came amongst us, that he might be the second Adam, who is the Lord from heaven; that as the first Adam by sin had ruined all those who are born of him after the flesh; so the second Adam might save all those who are born of him after the Spirit. And for this end, he has all power in heaven and earth committed to him; he has all fulness, yea, the fulness of the Godhead, dwelling in him, that he might be the head of the body the church; and that out of his fulness his members might be receiving grace in time, and glory in eternity.

Of this divine Person all the prophets have spoken since the world began; and what they have spoken in many words, the apostle sums up in a short description (Col. i. 15, &c.), where he is treating of that Person in the Godhead, who covenanted to come into the world to save sinners; "who is the image of the invisible God, the first-born of every creature; for by him were all things created, that are in heaven, and that are in earth, visible and invisible, whether they be thrones, or dominions, or principalities, or powers: all things were created by him, and for him, and he is before all things, and by him all things consist. And he is the head of the body the church: who is the beginning, the first-born from the dead, that in all things he might have the pre-eminence; for it pleased the Father that in him should all fulness dwell." In which words these three glorious truths are declared of Christ Jesus: first, that he created all things visible and invisible; secondly, that he upholds them all by the word of his power; thirdly, that he has redeemed unto himself a peculiar people through his own blood, who are his church, and he is to them what the head is to the body, the head of authority, the first in rank and dignity, and the head of influence, from whom life and motion and sense are communicated to all his members: for in him they live and move and have their being. In all things he is first, or has the pre-eminence; he is Jehovah, the Creator and the Preserver of all things, Jehovah incarnate, the Head of his church, and the Saviour of the body.

This is the blessed object of faith: and what can there be conceived beautiful, useful, or happy, what excellency is there or perfection, which is not in its highest degree in this most adorable God-man? What can a believer want, what can his heart desire, which is not here treasured up for his use? Here is a surety perfectly qualified, as man to act and suffer for man, as God to merit infinitely and eternally by what he did and suffered; and as God-man he has now all fulness of wisdom, and righteousness, and holiness, and strength, and everything needful for his people's happiness. Whither then should they go, but to him, for every grace and blessing? And to him they do repair, according to the command— "Look unto me, and be ye saved, all the ends of the earth." (Isai. xlv. 22.) The promise to them, who are looking unto him, is very extensive—" My God shall supply all your need, according to his riches in glory by Christ Jesus." (Phil. iv. 19.) By him they expect a continual supply of all their temporal and spiritual needs, and therefore on him they would have their eyes ever fixed, looking unto Jesus. While by faith their eyes are kept steady upon him, they will be discovering something new in this wonderful God-man, and receiving something out of his fulness, to strengthen their hopes, and to inflame their affections. He will grow more lovely in their sight, fresh beauties will discover themselves, new worlds of delight will appear: for all the glories of heaven and earth shine in their fullest lustre in his person.

The believer sees them at present: for by faith he can see him that is invisible: and although he has not such a perfect vision as they have, who standing round his throne see him face to face, yet he hopes to enjoy it soon: and he has even now this peculiar pleasure in viewing the glories of his God and Saviour, that he can truly say of him—" This is my Beloved, and my Friend," here I fix, and on him I rest; I want to look nowhere else for any good, since it all meets and centres in one object: for it hath pleased the Father and the eternal Spirit, that all fulness should dwell in the Son of God, and he is my beloved Saviour, and my dearest Friend; he is the Chief among ten thousand in my affection; yea, he is altogether lovely. The more I live by faith upon him, the more I love him; for I experience such tender compassion in his heart, and such a kind concern for me and my interest, that the love of Christ constrains me to love him again. He endears his person to me by continual favours. I do love him, but not so much as he deserves. I would increase, and abound more and more in love to him, as his mercies increase and abound to me; but a grateful sense of them, and love to him for them, are his own gifts, for which, as well as for his mercies, I must be content to be indebted to him for ever and ever. Lord! shed more of thy precious love abroad in my heart; enlarge it in true affection to thee, and make all that is within me bless thy holy name!

Reader, stop a little here and consider. Art thou one of these believers? Hast thou a warm heart for the person of Christ? Dost thou see in him, and in its highest degree, everything that is lovely; and art thou growing and abounding in love to him? If this be thy present happiness, thou wilt find many powerful motives to increase it in the 45th and 42nd Psalms. Read them, and see whether thou canst so mix faith with what is said in them of the incarnate God, as to conclude with David—"Whom have I in heaven but thee, and there is none upon earth that I desire besides thee?"

If thy heart be thus enamoured with his love, then thou hast got a key to the book of Canticles; for thou art the spouse of Christ. Mayest thou experience what is therein said of the glories of thy heavenly Bridegroom! and mayest thou grow in love to his adorable Person, by finding continual tokens of his love to thy soul in the several offices which he sustains for the dispensing of his favours! In these offices he is always endearing himself to his people. And this is the

Second thing, whereby the fathers in Christ grow in

the knowledge of him. There is not a want which sin has brought upon believers, but there is an office in Christ where it may be supplied; and the sense and feeling of that want, leading them to trust in him upon the warrant of his word and promise, will certainly bring them a supply in the hour of need. His offices are many, but they may be all included in these five. He is the Saviour, the Prophet, the Priest, the King, and the Advocate of his people.

The SAVIOUR, Jesus, a dear name, descriptive of his infinite grace, and sweetly suited to the sinner's wants. Whatever pollution or guilt he has contracted; whatever misery he deserves to suffer in time, or in eternity, Jesus is Jehovah, almighty to save him; for he was called Jesus, because he was to save his people from their sins. Whatever they stand in need of to make them happy,—wisdom, righteousness, holiness, comfort, or strength,—it is all in the fulness of Jesus freely promised, and by faith received, as it is written, "Ye are saved freely by grace, through faith," and saved for ever; for Jesus is the author of eternal salvation. The spirits of just men made perfect in glory are said to be crying with a loud voice, "Salvation to our God, who sitteth upon the throne, and to the Lamb, for ever and ever." So that the name Jesus is dear and precious to the saints in heaven; they are happily employed in ascribing the glory of their eternal salvation to the Lamb of God. And the believer has at present a part of their happiness; for Jesus is the Saviour. He can trust him for all the promised blessings of his salvation, and live by faith upon him for the receiving them. As every moment some of them are wanted, so the Saviour's love in bestowing them is more experienced; faith in him is thereby strengthened, and love to him increased.

And these graces will be continually growing, while the believer views the state of guilt and misery from which Jesus has saved him, the state of safety in which he has placed him, and the blessings which he has promised him in life and death, and in eternity. Must not such a Saviour become more precious for continuing day by day such free and unmerited benefits? And who can receive them, sensible of his unworthiness, without rejoicing in such a salvation, and admiring and adoring the goodness of the Saviour? O most blessed Jesus, increase the faith of thy people, that they may glorify thee more, by depending upon thee for all the promised blessings of thy salvation. Teach them how to do this as the great PROPHET of the house of God.

This is another of his gracious offices, suited to the ignorance of his people; for when sin separated them from God, they then lost the light of life, and had no means left in their own power to discover God and the things of God. Hear what two infallible witnesses say to this fact—"There is none that understandeth, there is none that seeketh after God." Mind, here is no exception, the prophet knew not one; neither did the apostle—"All the Gentiles had the understanding darkened, being alienated from the life of God through the ignorance that is in them, because of the blindness of their hearts."

To man in this state of ignorance, what could be so suitable as a prophet? And what prophet like him, who, being God, is possessed of infinite wisdom, and, being God-man, has that infinite wisdom for his people's use? He was made unto them wisdom, that by his divine teaching he might enlighten their understandings, and by leading them into all truth, might make them wise unto salvation. He begins his teaching by discovering to them their ignorance, which is a hard lesson to learn; but he uses such mildness and gentleness with his authority, that by degrees he subdues their pride, and makes them willing to sit at his feet to hear his words.

This is the humble posture of all his true disciples. They receive him by faith for their Teacher, convinced that without him they can learn nothing which belongs to their peace; and having been for some time under his teaching, they grow more sensible of their want of it. He discovers to them more of their ignorance, and thereby brings them to a closer dependence upon him for wisdom. And that is the way they rise in his school. Whoever is the most humble and teachable, he is the greatest in the kingdom of heaven. The abiding sense of his standing in need of the divine Prophet every moment makes him the highest scholar. And the Lord keeps him in this dependent state, waiting upon him for his continual instruction, in hearing and reading the word, and in prayer, for the enlightening Spirit to make the word effectual.

The great Prophet could teach without these means, but he has commanded us in the use of them to wait upon him; for in them he has promised to meet and bless his people, and for the fulfilling of this promise they wait. Christ's presence they look for in the use of all means, and they find it. He teaches them how liable they are to err, how little they know, how soon they forget; and thus they grow in a dependence upon, and in love to, their divine teacher. And as all the treasures of wisdom and knowledge are in him, and they can know at present but in part, they therefore will be waiting upon him for more—still more knowledge; and he answers his character—he teaches them wisdom. He shows them dangers, discovers to them the devices of Satan, guards them against the errors and heresies of the day, makes manifest the snares of the world, and in all respects fulfils to them the office of an infallible Prophet: for he keeps them from resting upon any false foundation, and enables them to build all their hopes of acceptance with God upon the atonement made by the High PRIEST of our profession, Christ Jesus.

This is his chief office. He is our Prophet to teach us our guilty, helpless state, and to bring us to rely upon him to save us from it by being our Priest. All we have sinned, and have incurred the pains and penalties due to sin. We are all justly liable to the sufferings and death, to the curse, and to the separation from God, threatened in his law to transgressors, and we have no means in our own power to escape them. How full then of grace and love was the heart of our blessed Immanuel, that he would vouchsafe to be a Priest to offer gifts and sacrifices for sin! His gifts were infinitely precious; he gave himself for us, the gift of his eternal Godhead, the gift of his immaculate manhood, body and soul, in which he obeyed perfectly, and so magnified the law, that it may be eternally honourable in admitting those who have sinned into heaven—the gift of his prevailing prayer for all that shall believe in him to the end of the world—and the gift of his body and soul to be once offered for sin, in the place, and in the stead of sinners, as it is written, "He suffered once for sins, the just for the unjust, that he might bring us unto God. He died for our sins according to the Scriptures. He was made a curse for us, that he might redeem us from the curse of the law, and that we who sometimes were afar off, might be made nigh by his blood, and might through him have access by one Spirit unto the Father." In these most precious gifts, in this everlastingly meritorious sacrifice, consists the office of our divine Priest; and upon him the believer rests. He is enabled upon this foundation to build all his hopes of acceptance.

The great atonement made by Jesus's obedience unto death is all his salvation and all his desire— all his salvation: for he looks nowhere else, but to Jesus and him crucified; he depends upon nothing else to save him from suffering and death, from the curse of the law, and from being eternally separated from God. And this is all his desire—to get a closer acquaintance and more intimate communion with the crucified Jesus. This is his one study and delight. I have determined, says he, to know nothing but Jesus, by whom I have now received the atonement. God forbid that I should glory, except in the cross of my Lord Jesus Christ. I would look upon all other things as dross and dung, compared to the excellency of the knowledge of that one offering, by which he hath perfected for ever them that are sanctified. In this his priestly office, bleeding and dying for me, he is beyond description, beyond conception, full of grace and truth; and daily he becomes more lovely in mine eyes. As I discover more of the exceeding sinfulness of my heart and life, my meritorious Priest grows more dear to me: I rest more safely on his atonement, satisfied of its infinite sufficiency to bring me near to God. And finding my faith and hopes established in it, and through it a free access to the Father, Jesus the sacrificed Lamb of God becomes day by day more precious to my heart. His blood and righteousness are the continual rejoicing of my soul. Oh! how happy am I in this my royal Priest; for now, even now, have I redemption in his blood, the forgiveness of sins—I am safe from the destroying angel under the blood of sprinkling, and I have also boldness to enter into the holiest, by the blood of Jesus. Daily do I experience more of the riches of his grace, comforting, strengthening, and sanctifying me through faith in his most precious blood. Through this he saves me from hell, through this he bestows upon me heaven, and for this shall be my song of everlasting praise. Unto him who hath thus exceedingly loved me, and hath washed me from my sins in his own blood, and hath made me, the vilest of sinners, a king and a priest (amazing grace!) unto God and his Father; to him be glory and dominion for ever and ever, *Amen*.

These are the breathings of the believing soul, now become well grounded upon the atonement, and living upon the priestly office of the Lord Jesus Christ, for peace and joy, and expecting to be established in them continually by his power, which makes another of his offices necessary; for some corruption or enemy, temptation or trouble, will be always trying to draw the eye of faith from looking unto Jesus, the High Priest of our profession; and such is the believer's helplessness, that he could not be fixed a moment, was not Jesus a Priest upon his throne, almighty to make all his enemies his footstool, and to rule in and over his people as their King.

In this relation he exceedingly endears himself to them; for they are in themselves weak and helpless. They are without strength to resist the least temptation, or to overcome the weakest enemy. They cannot of themselves subdue one corruption, or get the victory over a single lust. Neither can they perform one act of spiritual life. They cannot make nor keep themselves alive to God by any power of their own; for without Christ they can do nothing. Most mercifully then is his kingly office suited to their weakness. He is the great King over all the earth, as God; but he has a peculiar rule in and over believers as God-man, the Head of the body the church; to which he is connected by as close and near a bond, as the members of the body are with the head. He is the first in dignity, as the head is, and in all things has the pre-eminence; and what the natural head is to its members, the same he is to the members of his spiritual body; for he is the head, from which all the body, by joints and bands, having nourishment ministered, and knit together, increaseth with the increase of God. And for the ministering of proper nourishment and influence to his members, he has all power in heaven and earth in his hand. He is the Lord God omnipotent, whose kingdom ruleth over all.

It is not an outward thing, like the kingdoms of the world; but, says he, the kingdom of God is within you. He sets it up within, in the hearts of his people, and there he sways the sceptre of his grace, subduing all the evils within, and conquering all the enemies without, by his almighty arm. He takes them and theirs under his royal protection, and manages all their matters for them, until he bring them, by his power, unto eternal salvation. The power is his; but by faith it becomes theirs. When they find themselves helpless and without strength, then they look up to him to make them strong in the Lord, and by faith rest upon his promised strength, and thereby receive whatever degree of it is needful at that time.

Thus they live by faith upon their almighty King, and they glorify him by trusting in him for strength. By daily experience they become more sensible of their weakness, and learn to live more out of themselves upon him. They find the safety, the comfort of this. They see it is far better for them to be dependent upon Christ, that his power may rest upon them, than that they should be strong in themselves; and therefore they rejoice, they take pleasure in their own weakness, because it illustrates and magnifies the power of Christ, who does all for them and in them.

Hear one of these happy believers thus describing his case: I was caught up, says he, into the third heavens, into paradise, and I heard there unspeakable words, which it is not possible for a man to utter; and lest I should be exalted above measure, through the abundance of the revelations, there was given to me a thorn in the flesh, the messenger of Satan, to buffet me, lest I should be exalted above measure; for this thing I besought the Lord thrice, that he would take it away from me. And he said unto me, "My grace is sufficient for thee;" my grace is sufficient to sanctify this cross, and to support thee under it; it will be for my glory and for thy good it should be continued, because my strength is made perfect in weakness. The weaker thou art, the more will my strength be magnified in bearing thee up, until faith and patience have their perfect work.

This divine answer from my Lord and King satisfied me, and I have for fourteen years had sweet experience of the truth of it. I am a witness to the all-sufficiency of Jesus's grace; but never have I found so much of it as when I have been the most helpless in myself; and, therefore, most gladly will I glory in my infirmities and weaknesses, that the power of Christ may rest upon me, that his power may be continually glorified by my continually depending upon him for it, and that I may have fresh evidence of Christ's power working mightily in me. Since the Lord is thus become my strength, I take pleasure in infirmities, in reproaches, in necessities, in persecutions, in distresses, for Christ's sake, in whatever I suffer for him and his cause; for when I am weak, then am I strong—weak in myself, strong in the Lord; stronger in him, the more sensible I am of my own weakness; and then strongest of all, when finding I can do nothing, I live by faith upon him to do all for me. In this state of weakness and dependence I glory, I take perfect pleasure in it, because it honours the kingly office of my Lord Christ, and makes it plain to myself and others, that he keeps me every moment by his mighty power; for since I can do nothing, the excellency of the power which does all in me and by me, appears evidently to be of God, and not of man.

Reader, is not this a happy case? Is not that man blessed whose strength is in the Lord, and who can say in faith, Surely in the Lord have I strength? And what hinders thee from being as strong in the Lord as Paul was? Thou hast the same promises, the same God and Saviour to fulfil them; and, for thy greater encouragement to live upon him by faith, for the fulfilling of them to thee, he has another office, in which he condescends to be thy ADVOCATE, freely to take thy cause in hand, and to see it carried in the court of heaven. In this character he would represent himself, as having undertaken to answer all charges against thee, from whatever quarter they come, and to obtain for thee every blessing promised in his word, and for which thou appliest to him by faith in the time of need. In this amiable light he would have thee to consider him as thy days-man, to whom, being thy Saviour and thy Friend, thou mayest safely refer thy cause as the Mediator between God and man, who will transact all thy matters for thee with the Father, and as thy Intercessor, who appears in the presence of God for thee, that every blessing of his salvation may be thine. Under these names the Scripture describes the advocateship of the Lord Christ, which office he sustains for thy sake, to encourage thee to come with boldness to the throne of his grace. Thou hast a friend there, who is bound by his word, and also by his office, to see that thou want no manner of thing which is good; and although all things seem to make against thee, and thou canst find no human means of obtaining the promised good, which thou wantest, then look up to the Lord Jesus. Thou wilt glorify him at such a time, if thou canst trust in his intercession, and if the workings of thy faith be such as these:—

Although I am less than the least of God's mercies, a vile sinner, and to this moment an unprofitable servant, deserving for my very best works and duties to be punished with everlasting destruction from the presence of the Lord; yet glory be to his infinite grace, I have an Advocate with the Father, Jesus Christ the Righteous, and he is the propitiation for my sins. All the blessings which he has promised to give his dear people, as their Saviour, their Prophet, Priest, and King, he is my Advocate with the Father to obtain for me — a righteous Advocate, who asks nothing but what he has a right to, and who never asks in vain.

It hath pleased the Father, that all fulness should dwell in the Head of the body the church, and it pleaseth him that the members should, from the fulness of their Head, receive abundantly all the influence they want; for the Father himself loveth them, and out of his infinite love gave his Son to be their Head, that he might fill all in all of them. What, then, may not I expect from such an Advocate with such a Father? Already have I received so much, that I know Jesus appears in the presence of God for me. I can trust my cause in his hands. He has taught me to leave all my matters to his management, and I desire more simply to resign them up to him. I find everything goes on well which is left to his direction, and nothing miscarries but what I undertake without him. Oh, for more faith! The Lord increase it, that my precious Advocate may be more glorified, by my trusting him more, and that he may have all the honour of conducting my affairs, spiritual and temporal, in earth and heaven, in time and in eternity. Even so be it, Lord Jesus!

After the believer has been taught thus to trust the Lord Christ, and to expect that grace which in his several offices he is engaged to give, then his conversation will be well ordered: and as he daily grows in faith and dependence upon Christ, he will walk more in the comfort of the Holy Ghost: his outward as well as inward matters will come under the influence of grace, and will be left to the direction and government of the Lord Jesus, which is another excellency of the Life of Faith, and which renders it infinitely preferable to any other way of living.

The state of the case is this:—Christ has all power in heaven and earth given unto him. As God-man he has a mediatorial kingdom, which ruleth over all created beings and things; for they subsist by the word of his power, and are upheld by his providence: so that whatever, in his infinite love and wisdom, he sees best for his people, he is almighty to bestow it on them. They can want no promised good, nor suffer any outward evil, but he is able to give the one, and to deliver from the other. Their wants are many, their sufferings great. Sin has brought disorder upon the whole creation. The outward state of man in the world is full of misery, not only following him, but also in him, in his very frame and constitution. Pain, sickness, mortality in his body, emptiness in his enjoyments, disappointments, losses, worldly cares, something or other in body or estate troubling him; for man is born to trouble.

What manner of love then is this, that God our Saviour would take these things under his government, and manage them for the good of his people, whom he would have to be happy in him in this world, as well as in the next! He has given them many great and precious promises relating to the life that now is, and he is faithful who hath promised to supply their earthly wants, to sanctify their sufferings, and to make all things work together under him for their good. He has kindly undertaken their temporal, as well as their spiritual concerns; for nothing was left out of the covenant of grace. It was ordered in ALL things.

The outward state and condition of believers, their poverty or riches, health or sickness, trials of every kind, how great they should be, how long they should continue, are all appointed, and unalterably fixed; nothing left for chance to do. When the Lord God determined to bring many sons unto glory through Christ Jesus, the means by which he intended to bring them unto that end were in his purpose, as well as the end itself; therefore all things were ordered and made sure, even to the very hairs of their head; for they are all numbered. What a continual source of comfort is this to believers! Their present happiness is provided for as well as their eternal, in the covenant of grace. God is become their God, has made himself known to them in this covenant relation, and has thereby bound himself to give whatever he sees will be the best for them. But because he knoweth their frame, and how apt they are, under hard and long trials of faith, to be discouraged, he has therefore made them many sweet temporal promises for their support. Lest they should be weary and faint in their minds, he has engaged to deliver them from all evil: " Many are the afflictions of the righteous, but the Lord delivereth him out of them all." (Psalm xxxiv. 19.)

He delivers two ways, either by entirely removing the affliction, or by changing its nature; for he takes the curse out of it, and turns it into a real blessing; he makes it the means of increasing faith and patience, sweetens it with a sense of his presence, and demonstrates that it comes from love, by its increasing love to him in the heart of the righteous. This is the best deliverance, as one of the greatest sufferers for Christ witnesses, who, upon the mention of his afflictions, declares: " Out of them all the Lord delivered me," by saving me from the evil that was in them, and by making them yield the peaceable fruit of righteousness.

The Lord has also engaged to bestow upon believers all good:—" They that seek the Lord shall not want any good thing." (Psalm xxxiv. 10.) Their loving Shepherd will see that they lack nothing; no good thing will he withhold from them. To the same purpose are the promises in the New Testament (Matt. vi. 33):—Seek ye first the kingdom of God and his righteousness, and all these things, food and raiment, and all necessaries, shall be added unto you: I your God and Saviour, give you my word for it; trust me, and you shall never want. With confidence did he believe it, who said to the Philippians (iv. 19), " My God shall supply ALL your need, according to his riches in glory, by Christ Jesus."

What a powerful motive is here for the strengthening of our faith, that, be our wants ever so many, ever so great, our God has engaged to supply them all! We may boldly, then, cast all our care upon him, since he careth for us, and may rest assured of his managing our whole outward estate infinitely better than we could for ourselves. What trouble, what burdens, shall we be hereby eased of! What peace of mind shall we enjoy, when we can give up all our temporal concerns into the Lord's hands, and by faith see them all conducted for our good, by his infinite wisdom and almighty love! Blessed surely is the man, who thus putteth his trust in the Lord his God. He is delivered from the anxious care of getting, and from the fear of losing what he has got; he is easy about the present, the future he leaves to the Lord: his conversation is without covetousness, and he is content with such things as he has, and thereby escapes thousands of the common troubles of life.

In this sweet peace he enjoys his soul, because the Lord has said to him—"I will never leave thee nor forsake thee," in any state, in any want, or in any distress—I will be ever with thee to turn all things, seem they ever so afflicting, into real blessings. Trusting to this word, which cannot be broken, he may boldly say, The Lord is my helper, and I will not fear what man shall do unto me: let the world persecute me, my trade fail, poverty pinch me, sickness pain me, friends leave me, and all outward comforts forsake me, nevertheless I am a happy man. The Lord Christ is my portion, my all-sufficient portion still, and these things, being of his appointment, are for the best. I find them so, glory be to him! He makes them the means of weaning me from the world, deadening the old man of sin, bringing me to a more intimate acquaintance with himself, and to a greater experience of his goodness to my soul: whereby he enables me to trust all things for time and for eternity in his hands, who hath said unto me, and faithful is he that hath spoken, who also will do it, " I will never leave thee nor forsake thee."

But some may say, Are there any persons who live thus above the world, freed from its cares, and fears, and troubles? Yes, thanks be to God for his unspeakable gift. He has promised to make all things to work together for good to them that love him, and he has had witnesses in every age, of his faithfulness in fulfilling his promises. Read that little book of martyrs, Heb. xi., and you will see how happy they were in God, not only in prosperity, but also when all the world was against them. Great were the triumphs of their faith. They chose to suffer affliction rather than to enjoy the pleasures of sin for a season; they esteemed the reproach of Christ, and set more value upon it than upon riches and honours.

And we have a great cloud of witnesses in the New Testament, who rejoiced that they were accounted worthy to suffer shame for the name of Christ; who blessed their revilers, prayed for their persecutors, and took joyfully the spoiling of their goods. Hear one of them speaking the sentiments of the rest: "I account all things but loss, for the excellency of the knowledge of Christ Jesus my Lord, for whom I have suffered the loss of all things; and I do account them but dung, that I may win Christ." Still there are some among us of Paul's mind. The Lord hath not left himself without witness. We have a few names (may the Lord daily add to their number!) who can trust all their temporal affairs in the hands of Christ, and who find the happiness of having them in his management.

He does all things well for them; what would make them unhappy, he takes upon himself. "Cast thy burden on the Lord," says he, "and he shall sustain thee;" and he does sustain the weight of it, and thereby frees them from anxious care, and gives them sweet content. They have enough, let them have ever so little of outward things, because they have got the pearl of great price. Christ is theirs, and the Spirit of Christ enables them to make up all their happiness in him, and not in the things which perish in the using. Christ, with bread and water, is worth ten thousand worlds; Christ, with pain, is better than the highest pleasures of sin; Christ, with all outward sufferings, is matter of present and of eternal joy.

Surely these are the only happy people living. Reader, art thou not one of them? Art thou not a partaker of their happiness? If thou art a believer, it is thy privilege; thy title to it is good, and thou enterest into possession by faith; and if it be so weak that thou art not so happy as they are, thou shouldst take shame to thyself for dishonouring God thy Saviour, for robbing him of his glory before men, and for injuring thine own soul, by not committing all thy outward matters unto his guidance. What could he do more than he has done, to encourage thee to leave them to him, that he might manage them for thee? He has given thee argument upon argument, promises in abundance, bonds which cannot be broken, immutable things, in which it is impossible that God should lie, to convince thee that thou mayest safely trust in him for all temporal things which he knows will be for thy good.

Oh, pray then for more faith! Beg of the Lord to enable thee to walk more by faith, and less by sense, that thou mayest commit thy way entirely unto him, and he may direct all thy paths. The more thou trustest in him, the happier he will make thee. Therefore daily entreat him to deliver thee from taking any anxious thought for thy life, what thou shalt eat, or what thou shalt drink; or yet for thy body, what thou shalt put on. Since he knoweth thou hast need of all those things, and has sent thee to the fowls of the air, and to the grass of the field, to see what a rich provision he makes for them; art thou not much better than they? Oh! pray still for the increase of faith, that, all thy worldly matters being resigned and given up into the hands of the Lord thy God, thou mayest be eased of many weights and burdens, and mayest run with more patience and joy the race that is set before thee.

As these fathers in Christ learn by daily experience to live more upon him for the bread that perisheth, so do they for the bread that endureth unto everlasting life. They attain to a fixed, settled dependence upon Christ, for the conducting of all things belonging to their state of grace, to their comfortable walk in it, and to their finishing their course happily. They grow in the knowledge of those blessed truths, are more grounded and better established in them; and these, being received and enjoyed by faith, do manifest the excellency of living by it above any other state, except that of glory.

First, they are pardoned and accepted in the Beloved—in him partakers of every covenant mercy; for he was made of God unto them wisdom, righteousness, sanctification, and redemption. His whole salvation is theirs; and this is their state of grace, into which he has brought them, and by faith put them into the present enjoyment of it.

This was largely treated of before, but cannot be too much insisted upon, both because there is a growth in the knowledge of the covenant, and clearer evidence daily to be had of the believer's interest in it; and also because the love, and wisdom, and mercy in contriving, the power in executing, the grace in applying the blessings of the covenant, are all infinite. The height and depth, the length and breadth of those divine perfections cannot be fully comprehended. They surpass knowledge; so that if a believer knows a great deal of the way of salvation, yet there is still more, far more, to be known. So long as he lives, he must be learning, waiting upon the divine Prophet for his inward teaching, and he will become more dependent upon him, the more he learns: for the wiser he grows, the clearer views will he have of his having attained as yet but little wisdom, which makes him press forward. He believes that all the treasures of wisdom and knowledge are laid up in Christ, and he longs for more knowledge of his gracious undertakings, of his adorable person, and of his full and free salvation. He follows on to know the Lord. He advances from one degree to another, from faith to faith, and is not satisfied with any discovery until that which is in part be done away, and he shall know even as also he is known.

The believer being thus satisfied that he is in a safe state, looks up to the Lord to keep him, and to enable him to walk comfortably in it, which is another excellency of the life of faith. All things are well ordered in the covenant for every step he is to take: all treasured up in the fulness of Christ, and by faith received out of it. The believer has many enemies opposing him in his way

THE LIFE OF FAITH

heavenwards; but in Christ he has strength sufficient to conquer them all, and does conquer them. His worst enemy, that gives him most uneasiness, is indwelling sin, which is never at rest; like the troubled sea, always casting up some of its filthy motions and corruptions; so that when he is in prayer, it is ever trying to amuse and distract the mind with a thousand vain and idle thoughts, to weaken faith by its carnal reasonings and doubts; or when he is in any holy duty, it is ever present with him to hinder him from doing it so perfectly as he would.

Over this enemy there is no victory but by faith. The old man of sin defies all strength except that which is almighty; and therefore this the Lord has promised: and these believers had experience of his faithfulness whose iniquities he had pardoned, and who declared (Micah vii. 19), "He will subdue our iniquities." He will do it: He is engaged by promise, by office; it is his glory to save his people from the dominion of their sins. On him, therefore, they depend for continual victory; and according to their faith so it is done unto them. While they fight against sin, relying on the strength of their almighty King, they always conquer.

His arm subdues the strongest lust; but if they attack the weakest without him, they are infallibly conquered. And this has so often happened to those fathers who know him that is from the beginning, that now they never dare go down to battle but with their eyes upon the Lord. He has taught them to depend wholly upon him for the crucifying of the old man of sin day by day; and in the power of his might armies of lusts are made to flee before them. The Captain of their salvation encourages them to fight on, not only by subduing sin in them, but also by making this the earnest of their having in him an absolute mortification of sin. By faith they see it; and his victorious grace will never leave them until he put them into full possession of it.

Thanks be to God, through Jesus Christ their Lord, ere long they shall have perfect and everlasting victory over the whole body and being of sin. And as the old man is thus crucified, so is the new man quickened by the power of Jesus, received by faith, according to what is written,—"The just shall live by his faith." The justified person by his union with Christ is a partaker of the grace of life; and in virtue of this union he lives upon Christ, as a member does in the body, and thereby he has communion with the Father, by the bond of the Spirit: and this spiritual life is begun and carried on by faith; it is a life of faith; not as if faith quickened a dead sinner; for Christ is our life.

But the sense, and comfort, and strength of that life which Christ gives, are received by faith, and these are according as faith is. If faith be weak, so are they: as it grows, so do they. Which discovers to us another wonderful excellency of the life of faith, since by it we now partake of a spiritual and eternal life; "For he that believeth hath everlasting life;" hath it now—is already passed from death unto life; and he looks up to the Lord and Giver of it for everything needful, and expects it out of his fulness.

Hear one of these happy believers thus relating his case. I am dead to the law, says he, yet alive to God; I am crucified with Christ, and am a partaker of the merit and power of his cross; and by faith I have in him an absolute crucifixion of sin: and although the old man is thus crucified, yet the new man liveth; nevertheless, I live; yet not I. I live a spiritual life; yet not I as a natural man—I did not quicken myself; I cannot keep myself alive. Christ liveth in me; he is the Author of my life, and on him I depend for the continuance of it, in time and in eternity: for the life which I now live in the flesh, while I am in this body of sin and death, I live by the faith of the Son of God. He is the Author, he is the object of that faith, by which I have received life from him; by an act of sovereign grace he quickened me from a death in trespasses and sins, and united me as a living member into his mystical body; and I am kept alive through his living, acting, and working in me by his Spirit. He dwelleth in my heart by faith; and the more clearly I see this, the more do I love and enjoy the

Prince of life, my precious, above all expression, infinitely, eternally precious Jesus, who loved me and gave himself for me; that by his death I might be dead to sin, and by his resurrection might live to and with God for ever and ever. Thanks and praise be to thee without ceasing, thou dear Lamb of God, for thy love to me, the chief of sinners! Let all thy people say, Amen.

This is the happy case of those believers, who are, like the blessed Paul, strong in the Lord Christ. By his death they are dead to sin; and because he liveth, they are alive to God; for they who are joined to the Lord are one spirit. And as their faith increases, they have more spiritual fellowship with Christ in his death and resurrection; not only in the merit, but also in the efficacy of both. They grow more dependent upon the Lord's strength, and he daily mortifies in them the old man of sin; and as he grows weaker, their other enemies have less power over them.

By their lusts Satan tempts them; the more these are mortified, the weaker will be his temptations. By their lusts, by the lusts of the flesh, the lust of the eye, and the pride of life, the world tempts them; as these are subdued, they will be more crucified to the world. Christ living, dwelling, and reigning in them by faith, will day by day weaken the strength of sin, and Satan, and the world; and by the power of his death and resurrection he will be conforming them more to his own image and likeness. He will by faith enable them to be growing up into him in all things, as long as they live. They will be going on from strength to strength, till sin and death be swallowed up in victory.

Until that happy time come, he has appointed certain means, in the use of which they are to wait for the continual receiving of grace from him to deaden the old man, and for the growth of the new. And this grace they receive, not merely because they use the means, but because they use them in faith, expecting his presence in, and blessing upon them.

Believers set the Lord always before them, and look through the means at him; for without him they are good for nothing; but when observed according to his mind and will, as acts of trust in his promise, and of dependence upon his faithfulness, then they answer the end for which they were instituted, and become the means of spiritual communion with him.

And thus legal duties become Christian privileges. One of these means is attendance upon public worship, the ground and reason for which is Christ's promise, "Where two or three are gathered together in my name, there am I in the midst of them." Two or three believers make a church, when they are gathered together in the name of Christ's divinity. By faith they expect the fulfilling of his promise, and his presence in the midst of them; and they are then most spiritual worshippers when they are looking most unto Jesus, and enjoying communion with him. What are their prayers but acts of faith and dependence? "Whatever ye shall ask," says Christ, "in my name, believing, ye shall receive." Which words show us that prayer is nothing worth unless it be presented in Christ's name, and in faith relying on Christ's promise to hear and answer.

The object of prayer is the Godhead in three Persons. The address to each is in their covenant offices, and the petitions to each should be according as they stand related to sinners in those offices; and the communion with the divine Persons is thus expressed: "Through Christ Jesus we have an access by one Spirit unto the Father;" and whatever we ask, believing, we receive.

What is believers hearing the word? Is it not a continual dependence upon their divine Teacher, to make his word spirit and life unto their souls? They expect his presence, to enable them to mix faith with what they hear, and then they grow thereby. What is their keeping the Lord's day? Is it not to express their belief of his being risen, and entered into his rest? and of their having, by believing, entered into rest also? and therefore they wait upon Christ in the ordinances to keep them, until he bring them to his eternal Sabbath, to that rest which remaineth for the people of God. What is their attendance upon the Lord's supper? Is it not the communion of the blood of Christ, and the communion of the body of Christ, a real partaking by faith of his broken body, and of his precious bloodshedding, and of all the benefits of his passion?

In these, and all other ways of God's appointment, they expect Christ's presence, and therefore they go to them with gladness of heart to meet him. He is the dear object of their love, and he grows more lovely by every day's experience. They taste, and see more how gracious he is, and therefore to converse with him in prayer, and to be in his company in the ordinances, becomes more sweet and delightful to them. Oh! what happy moments do they therein spend! All the great, rich, and pleasant things in the world are less than nothing compared to this joy. Communion with Christ is heaven begun; and by faith they enjoy it, and nothing can rob them of it but sin; which makes them careful in their life and conversation to please their gracious Lord. They depend upon him to teach them his will, and to give them strength to perform it, that they may walk before him in all well-pleasing. Whatever is opposite to his will they dread, because it would deprive them of their greatest blessing, even communion with their best and bosom Friend.

Sin, viewed in this light, is blacker and viler than all the devils in hell. The love of Christ shows sin in its exceeding sinfulness, and faith working by love to Christ gains daily victory over it. He who has the love of Christ in his heart, will be thereby sweetly constrained to fight against, and powerfully enabled to conquer sin, so that it cannot separate him from his beloved Saviour, nay, it shall make him live in closer and nearer connection. The motions of sin within, and temptations without, to which he is continually liable, will show him the necessity of living in a settled dependence upon the grace and strength of the Captain of his salvation, who will lead him on conquering and to conquer, until he make him at last more than conqueror.

The same faith, working by love, has gained the hearts and affections of believers over to the interest of holiness, and the commandments now cease to be grievous. Love to Christ, who is perfect righteousness and holiness, cannot consist with the hatred of either; nay, they are renewed after his image in both, and renewed in knowledge, that they might know his precious image, and renewed in heart, that they might love it; therefore being thus created anew in Christ Jesus, they will certainly in the inner man delight in righteousness and true holiness. He has shed his love abroad in their hearts, has won them to himself, and now nothing is dearer to them than that everlasting righteousness by which he justifies them, and that true holiness of which they are become partakers in him, which they evidence by a holy walk, and in which he will present them holy, and unblamable, and unrebukable before the Father.

Thus he has perfectly secured the interest of holiness, and the glory of the most holy God; for they are his workmanship, created unto good works, to love them, to do them, to walk in them as the way to the kingdom; and they live by faith upon Christ's strength for will and power to do them, and upon his intercession for the acceptance of them, laying them all upon the golden altar that sanctifieth the gifts. Thus their whole dependence is upon Christ. He is all and in all of their Christian walk. To him they look for everything needful, to enable them to glorify God in their lives, and to show forth the virtues of him that hath called them; on his grace they rely, that their conversation may be as becometh the gospel of Christ, and that they may adorn the doctrine of God their Saviour in all things: and they find in him a sufficiency of grace; yea, they can do all things, and suffer all things, through Christ strengthening them.

Whatever difficulties they meet with in the way of duty, leaning upon their Beloved, he carries him through all. Whatever temptations, I will be with thee, says he; in the hour of temptation, look unto me, and thou shalt be saved. Whatever enemies, Fear them not, says he; for I am with thee, be not dismayed, for I am thy God, I will strengthen thee, yea, I will help thee, yea, I will uphold thee with the right hand of my righteousness. Whatever sorrows, Your sorrows, says he, shall be turned into joy, and your joy no man taketh from you. Whatever sickness, I will strengthen thee upon the bed of languishing, and I will make all thy bed in thy sickness. Whatever poverty, I will be a strength to the poor, a strength to the needy in his distress. Whatever persecution, Blessed are ye, says he, who are persecuted for righteousness' sake, I pronounce you, I will make you blessed.

Thus Christ is with them, and none of the evils or miseries of life can separate them from him. He keeps them safe, and carries them through all their trials by his mighty power, and they, trusting in him, find that he makes all things work together for their good. What a blessed life is this! surely there is none like it: for the life of faith is glory begun. The privileges, the happiness of it, are greater than can be described. The strongest believers upon earth may daily know more, and may experience far more of the comfort of walking by faith, because as they grow more established in it, they will be receiving more power over sin, and will walk nearer to God.

Having but one object to look unto, and to live upon for all things; here they will be quietly settled. What can so effectually keep them from being tossed to and fro, as to have all fulness treasured up for their use in Christ, and to be brought to a fixed dependence upon this fulness, and to live upon it for all things belonging to life and godliness? Hereby sweet peace will be established within, and there will be a regular walk in the outward conversation. The whole man will experience what the Lord has promised to his redeemed people, "I will cause them to walk by the rivers of waters in a straight way, wherein they shall not stumble." He leads them by his Spirit, and causes them to walk by the rivers of waters, where there are abundant streams of grace continually flowing, and he guides them in a straight way, that they shall not stumble or err therein; but shall be kept happily to the end of their course, and shall finish it to their everlasting joy.

And this is another inestimable privilege of believers. Christ has engaged to keep them unto the end; and having begun a good work in them, he has promised never to leave it until it be finished. What a strengthening is this to their faith, and what a glory does it put upon the whole life of faith; that it is a life which cannot perish? Believers have in them the immortal seed of eternal life! This is the crown of all: for how will this bear them up under crosses, support them in troubles, carry them on in their warfare against the flesh, the devil, and the world, and make them defy all dangers, yea, death itself! since they are assured from the mouth of God their Saviour, that none shall pluck them out of his hands. They do not trust themselves, or have any dependence upon grace received; but they rely upon the faithfulness and power of Jesus, who has given them abundant evidence that he will water them with his grace every moment, and hold them up by his strength, and they shall be safe.

How confident were believers of this in the Old Testament? One of them, who had attained this assurance of faith, says, "Surely goodness and mercy shall follow me all the days of my life!" and he with many others who had obtained like precious faith with him, declare— "This is our God for ever, he will be our guide even unto death." They were sure he would be their God, and would follow them with mercy, and guide them, and do them good in life and death.

To the same purpose our Lord has promised believers: "My sheep hear my voice, and I know them, and they follow me, and I give unto them eternal life, and they shall never perish, neither shall any pluck them out of my hand." How confidently did he trust in Christ for the fulfilling of this blessed promise, who said, "I am fully persuaded that neither death, nor life, nor angels, nor principalities, nor powers, nor things present, nor things to come, nor height, nor depth, nor any other creature, shall be able to separate us from the love of God, which is in Christ Jesus our Lord." Oh! sweet words of comfort! how happy was Paul in this assurance of faith! It is thy privilege, believer, as well as his. Thou hast the same promises that he had, the same God to fulfil them, and thy faith ought to be growing until thou be assured that no creature, not all the powers on earth, nor the gates of hell, can separate thee from Christ. They may as soon get into heaven and cut off Christ's right hand, which is impossible, as cut off one of the members of Christ's mystical body.

If thou art ready to say, I see clearly how I should glorify my dear Lord, and how happy I should be, if my faith was but like Paul's in this point, but I am so weak and liable to fall, and mine enemies so numerous and mighty, that I sometimes fear I shall never be able to hold out unto the end; because thou art such, therefore the Lord has given thee his promise that he will hold thee up, and thou shalt be safe. And this promise is part of the covenant, which is ordered in all things, and sure. Look at that, and not at thyself. Consider the Messenger of the covenant, in whom it is all ordered, and by whom it is sure. When thy unfaithfulness would discourage thee, think of his faithfulness. Let thy weakness remind thee of his strength. If indeed he leave thee a single moment, thou wilt fall; but he has promised, I will NEVER leave thee. If the number and strength of thine enemies make thee fear lest thou shouldst one day perish by the hand of Saul, he says to thee, thou shalt be kept by the power of God through faith unto salvation. But if thou art tempted to doubt, finding thy revolting heart apt to turn from the Lord, "I will put my fear," says he, "into thy heart, that thou shalt not depart from me."

Observe, it is his faithfulness and power, and not thine, which is to keep thee, and has covenanted to do it, and he has all power in heaven and earth, and he has given thee promise upon promise for the establishment of thy faith, that thou mightest be certain he will love thee, and keep thee unto the end. And when he has brought thee to a certainty of it, then thy comfort will be full. Christ will be magnified in thee, now he has made thee one of those fathers who have known him, that is, from the beginning. He has taught thee so to know him as to trust him for all things, and in all times. This is his crown and glory. He has enthroned himself in thy heart, as thy perfect Saviour, and his kingdom is within thee, even righteousness and peace, and joy in the Holy Ghost. Now thy calling and thy election is sure. Thou knowest that he is faithful who hath promised to keep thee, who also will do it. And having this assurance of faith, attended with the rejoicing of hope, and being sealed by the blessed Spirit to the day of redemption, surely thou art a happy man, thrice happy, whom the Lord has thus highly favoured.

How infinitely indebted art thou to his grace! Oh! what thanks and praises dost thou owe, more than thou canst ever pay, for what he has already done for thee! and yet this is only the dawning of the perfect day. His present favours are only earnests and pledges of what he will hereafter give thee. Therefore still trust in him, and he will enlighten thee more by his word and Spirit; he will enliven, strengthen, and establish thee more. Thy faith will daily rest more assuredly upon him; the joy of thy hope will increase, thy love will yet more abound. He will guide thee by his counsel in an even course, and will receive thee into glory.

Thus have I treated, as I was able, of the safety and happiness of living by faith upon the Son of God, and have described the common hinderances which stop its growth, and the victory over them, which the Lord gives his people. I have been forced to be very short, and could only throw out some hints upon this copious subject. May the good Lord pardon what is amiss, and bless abundantly what is according to his mind and will! If thou hast followed me, reader, in thy experience, and art indeed a happy believer, living upon thy blessed Jesus for his promised heaven, and for all things promised to thee in the way thither, think what a debt thou owest him! how dear and precious should he be to thy heart! He has saved thee from all evil, he will bless thee with all good. As surely as thou hast the earnest, thou shalt have the purchased possession.

Oh! what a Saviour is this! he has already bestowed upon thee the exceeding riches of his grace, but how great will be the riches of the glory which he will give thee? Thou wilt soon see him as he is, and then thou shalt be like him. No tongue can tell how great that glory will be, not all the tongues in heaven, after the number of the elect shall be perfected, no, not after they have enjoyed it for millions of ages; never, never will they be able to show forth all his praise for making them like himself. Surely, then, while thou art waiting for this glory which shall be revealed, thou wilt be going on from faith to faith, that thy beloved Saviour may become more dear to thee, and that thou mayest have more close and intimate communion with him. Every day's experience should bring thee to love his appearing more. Having tasted how gracious he is, thou shouldst be longing for the marriage supper of the Lamb with fervent desire. And being now a father in Christ, and strong in faith, thou wilt be often looking up to him, and saying,

Make haste, my beloved, and take me to thyself. Let me see thee face to face, and enjoy thee, thou dearest Jesus, whom my soul longeth after. It is good to live upon thee by faith, but to live with thee is best of all. I have found one day in thy courts, conversing sweetly with thee, better than a thousand; but this has only whetted my appetite; the more communion I have with thee, I hunger and thirst still for more. My soul panteth for nearer, still nearer communion with thee. When shall I come to appear before the presence of God? O thou Light of my life, thou Joy of my heart, thou knowest how I wish for the end of my faith, when I shall no longer see through a glass darkly, but with open face behold the glory of my Lord. Thou hast so endeared thyself to me, thou precious Immanuel, by ten thousand thousand kindnesses, that I cannot be entirely satisfied, until I have the full vision and complete enjoyment of thyself. The day of our espousals has been a blessed time. O for the marriage of the Lamb, when I shall be presented as a chaste virgin to my heavenly Bridegroom!

How can I but long earnestly for this full enjoyment of thy everlasting love! Come, Lord Jesus, let me see thee as thou art! Come, and make me like unto thee.

I do love thee, I am now happy in thy love, but not so as I hope to be. I am often interrupted here, and never love thee so much as I desire; but these blessed spirits standing now round thy throne are perfected in love. Oh! that I was once admitted to see as they do the glory of God in the face of Jesus Christ! Is not that the voice of my beloved, which I hear answering, *Surely, I come quickly!* Amen, say I, even so come, Lord Jesus. Make haste, my beloved, and be thou like to a roe, or to a young hart upon the mountain of spices.

Are not these, believer, the breathings of thy soul? Since the time for them is short, may they grow warmer, and more affectionate every day! Thou wilt wait but a little while before thou shalt see the King in his perfect beauty, and thou shalt be a blessed partaker of his eternal glory. And if he make these few lines any means of bringing thee to see more of his beauty at present, to live more upon his fulness, and to be happier in him, I hope thou and I shall, through his grace, meet him soon, and give him to eternity the glory of this and of all his other mercies. To the Lord I commend thee, on whom thou hast believed. May he strengthen and establish thy faith daily, that it may grow exceedingly, until he bring thee to the end of it, and admit thee into that innumerable company, who are ascribing blessing, and honour, and glory, and power to him that was slain, and hath redeemed them unto God by his blood! to whom, with the Father, and the Eternal Spirit, three Persons in one Jehovah, be equal and everlasting praise. Amen.